fast, stiff, sound and every way complete, for sale, at a great sacrifice. Address Yacht, Herald office

YACHT REBECCA FOR SALE.—SHE CAN BE SEEN at Greenpoint.

ASTROLOGY.

A BONA FIDE ASTOLOGIST, THAT EVERY ONE can depend on, is Madame WILSON. who tells the object of your visit as soon as you enter her room. Madame Wilson is without exception, the greatest astrologist that ever was known. She will invoke the powers of her wonderful science and tell all the events of your past, present and future life. and will warn you of danger and bring success out of the most perilous undertakings. Madame Wilson is also in possession of the celebrated magic charms No. 189 Allen street, over the bakery between Houston and Stanton streets. Charge for ladies and gentlemen, fifty cents.

ASTONISHING AND MOST WONDERFUL.—MADAME MORROW, seventh daughter, born with a caul and gift of foresight, tells how soon and often you will marry, and all concerns of life, even your very thoughts She guarantees those who visit her will not regret it. Fee 25 cents. 4 Ludlow, six doors from Houston street. Gentlemen not admitted.

CLAIRVOYANT.—MRS. SEYMOUR, MEDICAL CLAIRvoyant, rooms 210½ East Twentieth street, between first and second avenues. The most critical, medical and business consultations day and evening, and perfect satisfaction guaranteed always, or no pay.

MADAME RAY, NO. 260 SEVENTH AVENUE, NEAR Twenty-seventh street, surprises all who visit her. The sick, troubled and unlucky should test her power. She tells your very thoughts, lucky numbers, losses. Ladies 25 cents; gents, 50 cents

MRS. H. ROEDER, NO. 174 FOURTH STREET IS THE only true Clairvoyant, renowned Seer and gifted lady in this city. Revealer of all affairs through life, past, present, and future events; gives true and correct information on health, wealth, love affairs, journeys, law suits, difficulty in business, absent friends, sickness, &c. Thousands of visiters can witness the truth of her correct revelations during the past sixteen years Remember her residence, 114 Fourth street, near Tenth street.

N B—WHO HAS NOT HEARD OF THE CELEbrated Mme. PREWSTER, who has been consulted by thousands in this and other cities with entire satisfaction The fee s confident she has no equal. She tells the name of future wife or husband and that of her visiter. If you wish truth, give her a call at 251 Third avenue, above Twenty-first street Ladies, 50c ; gentlemen, $1.

THE GREATEST WONDER IN THE WORLD IS THE young and accomplished Madame BYRON, from Paris, who can be consulted with the strictest confidence on love, courtship, marriage, sickness, intemperance, situations, law suits, business, travelling, absent friends, lost or stolen property, &c She has also a secret to make you beloved by your heart's ideal, and bring together those long separated Residence No. 1 Mangin street, corner of East Grand, Williamsburg ferry. Ladies, 25 cents; gentlemen, 50 cents.

WHO WOULD NOT GO WHERE FORTUNE IS?—GO YE, see Miss WELLINGTON, the great English prophetess, the best of all, and cannot be excued Can be consulted personally or by letter, on all affairs of life, concerning law suits, journeys, absent friends, love, courtship, marriage, health, wealth, and who will reclaim drunken and unfaithful husbands. Miss W. is the only person in this city who has the genuine Roman and Arabian talismans for love, good luck and all business affairs, and are guarantees for life They ay not to consult this naturally gifted and beautiful young lady. Lucky numbers given. Highly respectable city references. Can be seen at her residence, 101 Sixth avenue, opposite Eighth street.

O ELDRIDGE STREET.—MADAME WIDGER, CLAIRvoyant and gifted Spanish lady, unveils the mysteries of futurity, love, marriage, absent friends, sickness, prescribes medicine for all diseases, tells lucky numbers, property lost or stolen, &c.

man, with plenty of milk, wishes a situation as wet nurse; has the best of city reference. Call at 126 2d av., from 1 to 4 P. M.

WANTED—A SITUATION, BY A RESPECTABLE young woman, as chambermaid and waitress, or to assist with the washing and ironing; no objection to go in the country; the best of city reference given, if required. Call at 123 West 33d st.

WANTED—A SITUATION, BY A RESPECTABLE young woman, as chambermaid and waitress or chambermaid and to assist in washing and ironing; the best reference from her last place for nearly nine years. Has no objection to go a short distance in the country. Call for two days at 432 7th av., near 37th st., rear house, second floor.

WANTED—BY A RESPECTABLE SETTLED WOMAN, a situation as good plain cook and to assist in the washing and ironing; has the best city reference from her last place. Call at 94 St. Mark's place, first floor, up stairs.

WANTED—A SITUATION, BY A YOUNG GIRL WHO never lived out, to assist in housework or to make herself generally useful. Call for two days at 266 1st ave., between 15th and 16th sts.

WANTED—BY A RESPECTABLE PROTESTANT girl, a situation as chambermaid and to do plain sewing; is willing and obliging; no objection to go a short distance in the country. Call at 81 25th st., between 6th and 7th avs.

WANTED—BY A YOUNG WOMAN, A SITUATION AS nurse and seamstress, or chambermaid, and would have no objection to go to the country with a family for the summer; can give the best of city reference. Call at 242 West 24th st., near 9th av.

WANTED—A SITUATION, BY A RELIABLE YOUNG man, as assistant bookkeeper and corresponding clerk, or as general clerk in a wholesale grocery; can furnish the best of city reference from last employer as to character and ability. Address J. C., box 193 Herald office.

WANTED—BY A RESPECTABLE PROTESTANT GIRL, a situation as chambermaid and nurse, and to do plain sewing or general housework, in a small private family; no objection going to the country as nurse. Call at 124 Bleecker st., near Wooster, for two days.

WANTED—BY A RESPECTABLE GIRL, A SITUATION to do housework in a small private family; best city reference. Call at 211 West 26th st., between 8th and 9th avs.

WANTED—BY A RESPECTABLE PROTESTANT young girl, a situation as chambermaid and waitress; no objection to go a short distance in the country; can operate on Wheeler & Wilson's machine. Can be seen for two days at 135 West 19th st., in the rear.

WANTED—A SITUATION, BY A RESPECTABLE widow woman, to cook, wash and iron; is a first rate baker; can get the best of city reference; has no objection to the country. Apply at No 2 Waldron place, between Bridge and Jay sts., in York st., Brooklyn.

WANTED—A SITUATION, BY A RESPECTABLE young woman; is a good cook, washer and ironer; the best of references given. Inquire for two days at 302 West 31st st., between 9th and 10th avs.

WANTED—A SITUATION AS CHAMBERMAID, OR TO do chamberwork and washing by a very capable young woman; best of city reference; no objection to the country. Call for two days at 333 9th av., in the store of T. Magee.

WANTED—BY AN AMERICAN GIRL, A SITUATION as chambermaid and laundress, or as child's nurse; has no objections to go in the country; can furnish good references. Call at 226 Sullivan st., room No. 16.

WANTED—BY A RESPECTABLE GIRL, A SITUATION in a small private family; is a good washer and ironer and an excellent baker. Can be seen for two days, if not engaged, at 252 6th st., near av. D.

have no objections to traveling with a lady or to attend stores. Call or address Miss Lennett, 523 West 23d st., below 10th av.

WANTED—BY A RESPECTABLE YOUNG WOMAN, situation as cook; she fully understands her business and is an excellent baker and pastry cook; is willing to assist in the washing if required. First class city reference; has lived four years in her last place. Apply at 107 East 13th st., near 3d av. Country preferred.

WET NURSE.—WANTED, BY A RESPECTABLE PROtestant married woman, a baby to wet nurse at her own house. Best reference. None but respectable families need apply. Call for two days at 310 West 27th st.

WANTED—BY A YOUNG GIRL, A SITUATION TO DO general housework; no objection to go a short distance in the country. Good city reference. Can be seen for two days at 222 West 50th st., between 8th and 9th avs.

WANTED—BY A RESPECTABLE YOUNG WOMAN, situation as cook. She is a good washer and ironer and has the best of city reference. Can be seen for six days at 120 20th st., between 6th and 7th avs.

WANTED—BY A RESPECTABLE YOUNG GIRL, situation as chambermaid and waitress; would be willing to go a short distance in the country. Can get good reference from her last place. Call for two days at East 29th st.

WANTED—A SITUATION, BY A RESPECTABLE young woman, to do chamberwork and waiting, or take care of children and do plain sewing or embroidery. Has the best of city reference from her last place. Call for two days at 186 West 26th st., between 8th and 9th avs.

WANTED—BY A RESPECTABLE PROTESTANT woman, a situation as cook in a private family; no objection to assist in the washing and ironing; is an excellent baker and would go a short distance in the country. Good reference can be given as to character and capability. Call at No. Gouverneur st.

WANTED—A SITUATION, BY A RESPECTABLE young woman, as waitress or chambermaid and to assist in the washing and ironing. Good city reference. Call two days at 321 1st av., between 19th and 20th sts., first floor, back room.

WANTED—BY A YOUNG GIRL, HAVING A WHEELER & Wilson's machine, a situation, or would like to work out by the month in a private family, or would be willing to assist in housework or to take care of a child, either in city or country. Best of reference given if required. Call or address 174 West 20th st., near 8th av., until suited.

WANTED—BY A RESPECTABLE WOMAN, A SITUAtion as cook in a first class family; understands French cooking in all its branches, ices, creams. Can give the most satisfactory references as to character and capability. Call for two days at 122 West 19th st., near 7th av.

WANTED—A SITUATION, BY A RESPECTABLE young girl as nurse and seamstress, who has good reference for six years; has no objection to go in the country. Can be seen for two days at 192 6th av., one door from 13th.

WANTED—A SITUATION AS CHAMBERMAID AND waitress in a private family. Best city reference from her last place. Call for one day at 217 Mott st.

WANTED—BY A RESPECTABLE GIRL, A SITUAtion as chambermaid or to do general housework in a private family. Reference satisfactory. Inquire at second house from the railroad office, corner of Flushing and Classon avs., Brooklyn.

WANTED—BY A RESPECTABLE WIDOW, A SITUAtion as seamstress; would be willing to take care of children or take the care of an invalid lady; no objection to travel; best of reference given. Call at 125 West 19th st., between 6th and 7th avs.; can be seen for two days.

WANTED—BY A COMPETENT PERSON, A SITUAtion as first class cook; best of city reference can be given from her last place. Can be seen for two days

WITHDRAWN

strange
red cow

Strange Red Cow

and other curious
classified ads from the past

SARA BADER

Clarkson Potter/Publishers
New York

Copyright © 2005 by Sara Bader

A list of credits appears on pages 201–203.

Published in the United States by
Clarkson Potter/Publishers, an imprint of
Crown Publishing Group, a division of
Random House, Inc., New York.
www.crownpublishing.com

CLARKSON N. POTTER is a trademark and
POTTER and colophon are registered trademarks
of Random House, Inc.

Library of Congress Cataloging-in-Publication Data
Bader, Sara.
Strange red cow: and other curious classified ads
from the past / Sara Bader.—1st ed.
Includes bibliographical references and index.
1. Advertising, Classified—United States—History.
I. Title.
HF6125.B33 2005
659.13′2—dc22   2004030466

ISBN 1-4000-5120-7

Printed in the United States of America

Design by Jennifer K. Beal

10 9 8 7 6 5 4 3 2 1

First Edition

For John

Contents

BOARD.—ROOMS TO LET, WITH BOARD, ON THE second and third floors, front, suitable for gentlemen and their wives or single gentlemen. Location unsurpassed. Apply at 118 West Twenty-third street References required.

BOARD.—TO LET, WITH BOARD, AT NO. 137 SECOND avenue, between Eighth and Ninth streets, one nicely furnished front Room, on second floor, and one on third floor, with secretary bedstead in each, on moderate terms for the summer. References exchanged.

BOARD.—A PLEASANT SUIT OF ROOMS TO LET ON second and third floors, separate or together, to gentlemen and their wives or single gentlemen. Dinner at 2 o'clock. Pleasant and desirable location. References exchanged Call for three days at 268 West Twenty-second street.

BOARD FOR ONE OR TWO GENTLEMEN, AT BEDford, Brooklyn, with a private English family. No other boarders Large garden, good stabling, pleasantly located in the country, with two lines of cars every five minutes. Address B , box 120 Herald office

BOARD AT 25 STUYVESANT STREET (CONTINUAtion of Astor place).—a gentleman and wife or two single gentlemen can be accommodated with Board, where the comforts of a home and choice of rooms secured, at the new English basement house east of Third avenue.

BOARD IN WEST SEVENTEENTH STREET.—ROOM, on second floor, to let, with Board, to a gentleman and wife or two single gentlemen House has all the modern improvements. Apply at 58 West Seventeenth street

BOARD IN HOBOKEN.—PLEASANT ROOMS, WITH Board, for gentlemen, at No. 1 Hudson Terrace, close to the erry.

BOARD IN HOBOKEN —HANDSOMELY FURNISHED Rooms, with good Board, are offered to three or four gentlemen, by a private family, on moderate terms; the house is pleasantly situated, very near to the ferry, and has all the modern improvements. Apply at 27 Union place.

BOARD WANTED—BY A GENTLEMAN AND LADY OF retired habits, in a small, quiet family, where there are no other boarders Board for the lady only. A furnished Room, with Bedroom, preferred. Address R. C. S , Herald office, stating terms, which must be moderate.

BOARD WANTED—FOR A LADY AND CHILD, IN the country, within thirty miles of New York, in a private family. Terms must be reasonable. Address or call on E. A. McMurray, 271 Pearl street, New York.

BOARDING.—A GENTLEMAN AND HIS WIFE AND two or three single gentlemen can be accommodated with good Board and well furnished Rooms, also a well furnished Parlor, by applying for two days at 242 Broome street, corner of Ludlow.

BOARDING —FURNISHED ROOMS, WITH OR WITHout Board, for gentlemen or ladies, at No. 9 Amity street, near Broadway.

BOARDING.—A FEW GENTLEMEN OR A GENTLEman and wife can be accommodated with good Board, where there would not be more than six or eight boarders, with most pleasant Rooms, and where the comforts of a home may be enjoyed. Terms moderate. Location 464 Eighth avenue, between Thirty-fourth and Thirty-fifth streets.

BOARDING.—A SMALL PRIVATE FAMILY CAN ACcommodate a gentleman and wife, or one or two single gentlemen, with a neatly furnished Room, on the second floor, and Board. The location of the house is fine, a few doors west of Sixth avenue. References exchanged. 88 West Thirteenth street

BOARDING.—SINGLE AND MARRIED GENTLEMEN will find handsomely furnished Rooms, in a house with all the modern improvements. In the immediate vicinity of the Second, Third and Fourth avenue cars. Apply at 400 Fourth street (Albion place).

BOARDING.—A GENTLEMAN AND LADY CAN BE accommodated with a fine Room on the second floor and full Board for the lady and partial Board for the gentleman. Apply at Mme. Yeoman's, 128 Greene street.

FURNISHED FRONT ROOMS—ON SECOND AND third stories, with full or partial Board, for two single gentlemen. All the modern improvements in the house. Apply at 228 East Broadway.

FURNISHED ROOMS.—TO LET, FURNISHED OR UNfurnished a very pleasant Room and Bedroom on first floor, fireplace and closet attached, in a private house, No. 254 West Twenty-ninth street Terms moderate.

FURNISHED ROOMS.—A PRIVATE FAMILY, OF TWO persons, would let three Rooms on first floor, communicating to a party of gentlemen, or a gentleman and wife for housekeeping. Apply at 402 Fourth street, Albion place.

GENTLEMEN AND THEIR WIVES, OR FAMILIES, can be accommodated with furnished Rooms, in suit or separate, at 178 West Fourteenth street; also single gentlemen; reference required; dinner at 6

GRAMERCY PARK, 80 EAST TWENTY-FIRST STREET. To let, suits of furnished Rooms, on second and third floors, suitable for families or single gentlemen; house first class; location very desirable for summer residence, between Lexington and Fourth avenues.

HARMONY HALL. 17 CENTRE STREET Gentlemen can be accommodated with nicely furnished Rooms, by the single night or week; rooms all newly fitted up. Apply as above.

HANDSOMELY FURNISHED ROOMS TO LET TO LAdies, without board, at 220 Sullivan street, near Amity.

HOBOKEN.—ONE OR TWO GENTLEMEN CAN OBtain Furnished Front Rooms, having a splendid view of the river, with partial Board, in the most delightful part of the city, within four minutes' walk of the ferry. Apply at No. 6 River terrace.

HOME COMFORTS—VERY DESIRABLE ROOMS, with Board, can be had at 161 East Eighteenth street, by gentlemen and their wives and single gentlemen; no objection to children; location excellent.

LARGE, DESIRABLE NEWLY FURNISHED ROOMS to let, with Board, at 384 East Fourth street; location central, one block from Broadway; references exchanged.

MRS. M. B. SUMNER, No. 22 WEST TWENTY-NINTH STREET. A Parlor on first floor, and two single Rooms to let, with Board. Table and style of housekeeping unexceptionable.

NO. 56 EAST TWENTIETH STREET, CORNER OF Fourth avenue, second door from Gramercy Park to let. Handsomely furnished Rooms in suits or single, with private table or without Board; a pleasant location for gentlemen who prefer taking their meals at a hotel.

NEW YORK BOARD AGENCY, 62 EAST FOURTEENTH street, Union square.—Persons wishing Rooms, with or without Board, directed without charge Those having rooms to let should register them at once.
E. LAWRENCE & CO.

NO. 77 EAST FIFTEENTH STREET, NEAR IRVING place—Suits or single Rooms to let, with Board, furnished or unfurnished. House first class; location desirable, within one minute's walk of Union square, the Academy of Music and the Medical College.

ONE OR TWO GENTLEMEN CAN HAVE SUPERIOR accommodations in a private family of young people, up town, on very moderate terms, to agreeable parties; house first class; modern improvements. Address, with reference, Broadway, box 196 Herald office.

PERSONS DESIROUS OF OBTAINING GOOD BOARD and pleasant Rooms can be accommodated by applying at No. 77 Fourth avenue, near Tenth street, one block from Broadway. House first class, and has all the modern conveniences.

PLEASE NOTICE.—PARTIES LOOKING FOR FIRST class accommodations and pleasant airy Rooms for the summer, will find such at 135 Madison avenue, corner of Thirty second street Stages and cars running near and by the house. Terms reasonable.

66 Place your wants in these columns and they will be 'a light set upon a hill that cannot be hid.' **99**

—FEBRUARY 24, 1892, *DAILY NEBRASKA STATE JOURNAL*

Going to Market

The Angler

The Country Squire

About This Book

I came to appreciate the classified advertisement by chance, just a few years ago, while researching a documentary on the Declaration of Independence. My research brought me to the microfilm room at the New York Public Library where I scanned eighteenth-century newspapers looking for clues that could help tell the story of our nation's treasured document. There I was, making my way through 1776, one page at a time, when I spotted this ad:

> CAME to my plantation, in Springfield township, Philadelphia county, near Flour-town, the 26th of March 1776, A STRANGE RED COW. The owner may have her again, on proving his property, and paying charges.
>
> PHILIP MILLER.
>
> —May 1, 1776, *Pennsylvania Gazette*

While it didn't say much about the Declaration of Independence, it did say something about a man named Philip Miller and what life was like in Springfield Township in the spring of 1776. I pictured Mr. Miller discovering that stray cow on his plantation, sizing her up, and checking for any identifying marks. Perhaps he went straight home, sat down at a writing table, and with the tip of his quill wet with ink, composed those lines. I've worked on historical reenactments, so I might be quick to dress a set, but those few simple lines transported me back in time more quickly than any formal document or history textbook could.

Philip Miller's ad got me thinking about classifieds, past and present. Like him, many of us, for one reason or another, have put our faith in those small boxes of text. We've scoured the columns, some of us religiously, for good jobs, new lovers, lost pets, used cars, secondhand stuff, better living arrangements, upcoming garage sales, and various other day-to-day needs and wants. And over the years, we've contributed our share of advertising to the pool of offerings. According to the Newspaper Association of America, classified advertising in the country's daily papers raked in more than $16 billion in 2004 alone.

But though classifieds are clearly a useful tool in our lives—some might argue essential—we rarely file them away for future reference. Like a "to do" list, a column's practical relevance can fade by the day. Such a short-term life span blesses the format with a precious low profile, at least historically speaking. The average advertiser composes a notice for the here and now, paying no attention to the document's potential archival value. Indeed, because postings are time-sensitive, they make known immediate desires with particular clarity. It is that sense of immediacy—a scene as simple and as complicated as a man with a trespassing cow on his hands—that inspired me to look for more.

When I set out to dig up vintage ads, I didn't know the character of the trails I would travel or the content of the postings I would find along the way. I did mark out particular plots for excavation—Richmond, Virginia, during the Civil War, for example—but I also roamed freely and let the ads lead the way. With the "strange red cow" in my mind's eye, I looked forward to excavating and reassembling a lost and found section. Other categories organically fell into place: personals, information wanted, help wanted, swaps.

What I wasn't prepared for was the number of runaway-slave advertisements that saturated the columns of eighteenth- and nineteenth-century newspapers. You can't move very far in any one direction without coming across one of these notices, written and posted by owners, overseers, jail wardens, and others when a slave couldn't be accounted for or was found somewhere en route. We have come to think of the classifieds as the people's marketplace. In the late nineteenth century, the *Rockland Courier-Gazette*, a Maine newspaper, referred to its advertising section as "Everybody's Column"; in the early twentieth century, the *Marion Daily Star,* an Ohio paper, coined it the "People's Column." Indeed, the classified section has evolved into a profoundly public bulletin board. But it wasn't always that way. For slaves living in America, the notice columns belonged to their masters, who sought, bought, and sold them through the printed word.

The classifieds chosen for this book have been lifted primarily from newspapers, but also a handful of magazines, booklets, and online sources, all published in America over the last three hundred years. Ads reproduced as they originally appeared give us a sense of how their first readers experienced them; all others have been reset with an eye to preserving archaic grammar, spellings, and, indeed, typos. For every advertisement included, there are thousands I could have selected and millions more that I have yet to discover. This compilation is a personal tour, based on the regions and time frames I chose to research. New York City served as my main base camp, though I ventured as far west as California and as far south as Florida.

As this book goes to press, the classified archive continues to grow: Every day brand-new postings are created—online and on paper. With such a plentiful resource in perpetual growth, an exhaustive collection of classifieds can never exist. In the pages of *Strange Red Cow,* I present a sample. The ads here are organized by category, then broken down further into brief vignettes. Each cluster of ads, set into context with commentary, reveals a chapter of the larger American story. From the same newsprint that lined cupboard shelves, lit the evening fire, and helped housebreak puppies comes an intricate map of cultural history.

Nightingale	Cat	Eagle	Greyhound

Sparrow

Squirrel

Jack come and see.
Two Owls in a Tree.

Hare

Auricula

Queen of the May

Cow

Ostrich

Oak

Introduction

Long before any of the notices included in *Strange Red Cow* appeared in newsprint, long before a newspaper was ever established in Europe or in the American colonies, or before the first printing press for that matter, practical day-to-day needs and wants still found ways to make themselves known. Walls unearthed in the ruins of Pompeii, for example, recorded crudely painted announcements (a testament to the rising literacy rates in ancient Rome), among them listings for local house rentals.

In England, the first known handwritten notices appeared in the fifteenth century, posted in well-trafficked public locations for maximum exposure. Scribes made a living penning these announcements, known as *Siquis,* meaning "If anybody" in Latin, a term borrowed from Ancient Rome, where public notices often began with the two words *Si quis* ("If anybody knows of . . .").

In Mainz, Germany, Johannes Gutenberg invented printing from movable type around 1450, and by 1476, William Caxton had established a print shop in England. In the seventeenth century, newsbooks—pamphlet-sized publications that disseminated news of the day in various European countries—printed early examples of "want ads." King Charles II, an avid pet owner, was known to regularly advertise in *Mercurius Publicus* when any of his dogs, hawks, or falcons went astray. One such ad, a notice for his missing "Smooth Black Dog, less then a Grey-hound," ran in June of 1660. Apparently it met with little success, though, because just a week later, this notice appeared: "We must call upon you again for a Black Dog, between a Greyhound and a Spaniel, no white about him, onely a streak on his Brest, and his Tayl a little bobbed."

The first official newspaper published in the English language was the semi-weekly *Oxford Gazette*. The debut issue was "Published by Authority" on November 16, 1665. Just a few months later, the newspaper moved its headquarters to the country's capital and changed its name to the *London Gazette*. Initially, advertisements were banned from the publication on the grounds that such notices were "not properly the business of a paper of intelligence." Only postings relating to "matter of state" were permitted. But it wasn't long before advertisers were scouting for their lost and stolen property in the pages of the *London Gazette*.

Although the printing press was established in colonial America in 1638 (set up at Harvard College in Cambridge, Massachusetts), it took more than half a century before Benjamin Harris, a London bookseller who emigrated to Boston, tried his hand at publishing a newspaper in serial format. On September 25, 1690, Harris published the first issue of *Publick Occurrences Both Forreign and Domestick*. It was four pages long, the last page left blank, supposedly so that readers could jot down their own newsworthy notes before passing it along to others. The top paragraph outlined his long-term plans for the paper: "the Countrey shall be furnished once a moneth (or if any Glut of Occurrences happen, oftener,) with an Account of such considerable things as have arrived unto our Notice." But those plans didn't have a chance to play out. The content of that first issue did not sit well with colonial authorities (Harris insulted the Iroquois, allies of the English, and accused the King of France of sleeping with his son's wife). The Governor and Council suppressed the paper just four days after its debut, claiming that it had been issued "without the least Privity or Countenance of Authority" and "that therein is contained Reflections of a very high nature: As also sundry doubtful and uncertain Reports." Authorities recalled the circulating issues, which is why original copies are so scarce today. The National Archives in London holds the only known surviving copy.

For the next fourteen years, the colonists continued to gather their news as they had for some time. They received dispatches verbally from town criers and from each other. They read locally printed broadsides, as well as English newspapers, brought over by ship captains and circulated in public coffeehouses and taverns. And for some notable colonists, private handwritten newsletters supplied information about affairs both foreign and domestic. It's not surprising, then, that the first successful newspaper in the colonies was the *Boston News-Letter,* published by John Campbell, then the postmaster of Boston and the author of a number of those handwritten newsletters. "From Monday April 17 to Monday April 24, 1704" was the date noted at the top of the first issue. This time, the words "Published by Authority" appeared clearly below the title. It began as a two-page publication, the front and back of a half sheet of paper. America's first newspaper classified ad appeared in that debut issue, the last item printed on the back, and posted by John Campbell himself:

Advertisement.

THis News Letter is to be continued Weekly ; and all Persons who have any Houses, Lands, Tenements, Farmes, Ships Vessels, Goods, Wares or Merchadizes,&c. to be Sold, or Lett ; or Servants Run away ; or Goods Stoll or Lost, may have the same Inserted at a Reasonable Rate ; from Twelve Pence to Five Shillings and not to exceed : Who may agree with *Nicholas Boone* for the same at his Shop, next door to Major *Davis's*, Apothecary in *Boston,* near the Old Meeting-House.

All Persons in Town and Country may have said News-Letter Weekly upon reasonable tearms, agreeing with *John Campbell* Post-Master for the same.

Campbell's ad worked. In the next issue, a subscriber placed a notice for two lost anvils. By the third installment, those two ads were joined by a posting for stolen clothing and America's premier real estate advertisement, the offer to sell or lease property on Long Island's Oyster Bay.

But though a handful of subscribers responded quickly and enthusiastically to Campbell's posting, the advertising section grew slowly and took years to truly get under way. That sluggish growth can be attributed, at least in part, to the newspaper's small circulation, which at first was limited to 250 copies and targeted not the general public, but literate, well-to-do New Englanders. Surely subscribers must have shared their copies, but it still took time for the readership base to expand significantly. And it took time for colonists long used to tacking up their "wants" on the local signpost, at the courthouse, or on the church door, to believe in and depend on the benefits of the notice columns.

The *Boston News-Letter* was the only newspaper distributed in the colonies until 1719, when the *Boston Gazette* appeared as competition. By 1765, eleven out of the thirteen colonies had newspapers (Delaware and New Jersey were the exceptions), and some colonies could boast of more than one title. In total, twenty-three weekly newspapers circulated in print. By the mid-eighteenth century, advertising inserts had become a popular feature of the layout, often appearing on the back page of the newspaper under one simple heading, "Advertisements." We know them now as "classifieds," ads organized by category, but the newspaper industry didn't start using that term until some time after the Civil War. By then, with so many notices printed daily in the newspaper, the section clearly required diligent classification.

HARE

SWAN

DUCK

WIND-MILL

COW

JOCKEY

Tent	Black Bird	Crown & Cushion	Sampfon	Oak
Nuts	Pilgrim	Griffin	Oftrich	Peftle and Mortar
Saw and Mallet	Water But	Cock	Afs	Raree Show
Turnips	Fox	Porter	Swan	Dung Barrow
Sailor	Sky Lark	Bell	Pig	Artichoke
Weather-cock	Elephant	Rofe	Turk	Sparrow
Wheatfheaf	Huntfman	Anchor	Squirrel	Cottage

CHAPTER I

Lost and Found

> ☞ Loſt on the 10. of *April* laſt off of Mr. *Shippen*'s Wharff in *Boſton*, Two Iron Anvils, weighing between 120 and 140 pound ach : Whoever has taken them up, and will ʒring or give true Intelligence of them to *fohn Campbel* Poſt-maſter, ſhall have a ſuffi- cient reward.
>
> —April 24—May 1, 1704, *Boston News-Letter*

In the large family of classified advertising, the lost and found advertisement stands out for its sincerity. Born out of the simple desire to reclaim or restore property, it is typically a genuine plea to the public that, even three centuries later, still resonates. Indeed, everyone can relate to the empty feeling of having lost *something*—a set of house keys, a dearly loved pet that strayed too far, or an irreplaceable family locket—and we all know the surge of relief that accompanies the safe return of an important belonging. People lose and find things every single day and, fortunately, bits of that history are recorded in our classifieds.

Lost and found notices leave behind a trail of artifacts, a catalog of possessions used over the last three hundred years. Pulled from the columns of countless pages, these postings tell us much about the shape, color, and relative value of our material past. There for the taking are precious historical details that require no fact checking: what a snuff box was made out of, the fabric used to line a nineteenth-century cloak, the contents of a soldier's Civil War saddle bag, or the color of a 1949 Girl Scout pencil. But step back from this frenzy of detail and wider patterns of shifting cultural attitudes emerge.

The ad for the missing anvils, the colonies' first lost and found insert, offers clues and raises questions. At more than a hundred pounds apiece, those tools didn't fall out of someone's pocket. They were difficult to transport, and the typical colonial-era blacksmith owned only one, maybe two. So how did two anvils go missing and who placed the ad in the newspaper for them? Did one or more blacksmiths leave them behind, perhaps while moving from one site to another? Or did a merchant import the tools from England, only to lose track of them on a Boston dock? What we do know is that a man named John Campbell, then the postmaster of Boston and the publisher of the *Boston News-Letter*, agreed to serve as the ad's designated point person. His office doubled as a local lost and found department, where a finder could "bring or give true Intelligence" of found property, then collect "a sufficient reward."

The reward set aside for the anvils was probably hefty: they were expensive to purchase, and critical to the growth of the colonies. An anvil made it possible for a smith to fashion any number of practical objects. With it, he could craft knives, forks, rakes, shovels, nails, hooks, latches, candlesticks, chains, hinges, scythes, anchors, metal rims for wagons, shoes for horses and oxen, and almost anything else made out of metal that a colonist might need. He could also make and mend tools for his customers. But without an anvil—or a ready supply of flat smooth rocks—none of that work was possible: doors couldn't be hung, fields couldn't be plowed, and nails simply wouldn't exist. What was once a costly and necessary item in any thriving colonial community holds little practical relevance for most of us today.

Tools and other functional wares played a starring role in early lost and found inserts. Stray pieces of finery also turned up—jeweled items, fancy watches, silver spoons, high-end imported fabrics, etc.—but eighteenth-century Americans depended heavily on their utilitarian belongings. Each posting is a fragment of material history unearthed; pieced together, a vivid picture of rustic eighteenth-century living takes shape.

WAS LOST, between Philadelphia and the Black-horse, on Lancaster road, a bundle of SOAL LEATHER, containing six sides. Whoever finds the same, and delivers it to Lieut. Col. Caleb Parry, Ferry-keeper, on Schuylkill, or to the subscriber, or gives information where it may be had, shall have TEN SHILLINGS reward, paid by JACOB HINKLE.

N.B. Shoemakers and others are desired to take notice if said leather should be offered for sale. March 9, 1776.

—March 27, 1776,
Pennsylvania Gazette

WAS FOUND lying in the street, a little before the British troops came into this city, a BOX of cross-cut SAWS. The owner proving his property and paying charges may have them again, by applying to JONATHAN EVANS, in Second-streets.

—December 10, 1778,
Pennsylvania Packet

lost and found

> LOST, yesterday, between the meeting-house in Worcester, and the road leading to Hardwick, a pair of SADDLE BAGS, containing a Cheese, some pulled Sheeps Wool, a number of Apples, a striped small Apron, and a small pair of blue Stockings. Whoever has found the same, and will leave them at the Printing-Office in Worcester, or deliver them to me in Hardwick, shall be handsomely rewarded by JOSEPH BERNARD. Decem. 24th.
>
> —December 25, 1777, *Massachusetts Spy or, American Oracle of Liberty*

> FOUND last week, a pair of SADDLE-BAGS, containing a number of Apples, and other valuable *eatables*, &c. Enquire at Mrs. Jones's, inn-holder, Worcester.
>
> —January 1, 1778, *Massachusetts Spy or, American Oracle of Liberty*

A sense of closure is usually absent from lost and found advertisements. Occasionally, however, a subsequent posting provides another layer to the story. These ads ran one week apart, and by all appearances, seem to refer to the same set of saddle bags. We can only hope that Joseph Bernard read his local newspaper on New Year's Day of 1778.

Although only a fraction of what Americans lost or found ended up as notices in the newspaper, the ones that did make it into print link us to the men and women who wrote those words and the people who happened to spot them in the paper that day. In just a few sentences, it's suddenly possible to get a glimpse of an era, to witness, at least for just a moment, the habits and concerns of those who lived it. We can untie the twine that once wrapped up their parcels, rifle through satchels, empty out coat pockets; with a little imagination, we can sort through it all and practically touch the contents. If we strain to identify with those who commuted in

strange red cow

LOST at the late Fire, two leather Buckets, marked W. PLUMSTED & Co. one Ditto, marked E. SHIPPEN & Co. one ozenbrigs* Bag, marked A R & Co. one Ditto, marked W P & Co. two Ditto, marked S A & Co. one ditto, marked R S & Co. Whoever brings them or any of them to John Armit, in Front street, shall be satisfied for their Trouble.

—February 2, 1742,
Pennsylvania Gazette

FOUND, the Beginning of March last, between *Coultas's* Ferry and *Schuylkill* Mill, a Bundle of Compasses. The Owner, describing them, and paying Charges,† may have them again, by applying to *Richard Meggs*, at Mr. *Andrew Hamilton's* Plantation, near the *Lower Ferry*.

—May 2, 1745,
Pennsylvania Gazette

FOUND, on the Eighth Day of this instant** September, in a hollow Tree, on the Plantation of Francis Wayne, and now at his Dwelling house, in East-town, Chester County, several fine Hats, a Woman's Beaver Hat, a Cutlas, a Thickset Coat, two Saddles and Bridles, Half a Side of curried upper Leather, a small Keg, with some Powder in it, and several small Matters of Hard-ware. The Owner, or Owners, proving their Property, and paying Charges, may have them again.
FRANCIS WAYNE.

—September 11, 1760,
Pennsylvania Gazette

Brandywine, September 29, 1772. WAS FOUND in the possession of a boy, last Friday, the 25th instant, a pair of large SILVER SPURS, which are supposed to be stolen. Any person applying to the subscriber, proving the marks, and paying the charge of this advertisement, may have them again, at the Royal Oak Tavern.

PETER VANDEVER, junior.

—October 7, 1772,
Pennsylvania Gazette

---

* Ozenbrigs: an inexpensive linen, typically worn by slaves and indentured servants. The name comes from Osnabrück, Germany, where this kind of material was originally manufactured.
† The frequent reference to "paying charges" spoke to the cost of inserting the notice in the newspaper, a fee initially incurred by the advertiser, but generally reimbursed by the owner of the lost goods.
** The word *instant* (or the abbreviation *inst.*) appears often in eighteenth- and nineteenth-century advertisements and indicates the current month. *Ultimo,* or *ult.,* refers to the previous month.

lost and found

horse-drawn carriages and depended on candles to light their corridors, these ads can personally introduce us. They had good days and bad days; they got distracted, disorganized, and like us, left important things behind. That our collective ancestors forgot their books in carriages, left their capes on battlefields, and dropped their keys and their cash is oddly reassuring. We are still losing our stuff today, though what we own and wear and carry with us—and what we decide to return and retrieve—inevitably changes over time.

A Curious Moment in Classified History

In 1736, the colony of New Jersey hired Benjamin Franklin, a reputable and accomplished printer, to generate £50,000 worth of local paper money. That summer, Franklin relocated to Burlington, New Jersey, where he went to work printing those bills. Apparently, on his return trip to Philadelphia that September, he lost some of his printing supplies. The following week, he did the sensible thing, and ran this advertisement in his own newspaper.

LOST laſt Week in removing the Printing Preſs, and either left on the Wharff at *Burlington*, or dropt off the Dray between the Waterſide and the Market in *Philadelphia*, A Pine water-tite Trough, containing ſundry odd Things and Utenſils belonging to the Preſs. Whoever brings it to *B. Franklin* ſhall have *Five Shillings* Reward.   *Philad. Sept.* 16. 1736.

—September 9–16, 1736, *Pennsylvania Gazette*

VICTORIAN OBJECTS OF DESIRE

Before the Industrial Revolution took hold of America, things were made by hand. The concept of disposable goods, now common-place, was simply inconceivable back then. Not only were a baby's diapers (known then as *napkins* or *clouts*) washed and used again and again, each one was sewn by hand from pieces of absorbent mate-rial (the name *diaper* actually comes from the diaper linen once used to make them). Even something as small as a button, easily replace-able today, could have been worth its weight in gold or silver.

FOUND by a Negro Boy, between Messrs. Grimké and Rowand's plantations, *a Gold Sleeve Button*. The own-er describing the same, paying for this advertisement, and giving the boy a trifle for his honesty, may have it again on applying, at Stono Bridge, to   JOHN JACKSON. ‡

—June 18, 1778, *South-Carolina and American General Gazette*

The Industrial Revolution expanded our material inventory and our material appetite. The era of handmade goods gave way to mass production. Factories churning out everything from shoes to clocks to plows enticed many Americans to trade their work on the farm for better-paying industrial jobs in or near metropolitan centers. Cities grew in size as these rural transplants were joined by a steady flow of newly arrived immigrants. Class formations took shape: the hardworking labor force that made factory pro-duction possible, wealthy industrialists who reaped the biggest fi-nancial rewards from the market economy, and a growing middle class of business owners, lawyers, doctors, teachers, and other white collar professionals.

Roam through nineteenth-century lost and found postings, particularly those that ran in big-city dailies, and you will inevitably run into the seemingly boundless material culture associated with this growing middle class. The Industrial Revolution sparked a consumer economy, and the middle-class American, with money in hand and thousands of new products to spend it on, was a perfect customer. Obsessed with gentility, physical appearance, and

LOST — LEFT IN THE LADIES' DRESSING ROOM, Academy of Music, Thursday evening (Light Guard ball), a white merino Opera Cloak, white silk lining, bordered with swan's down. A liberal reward will be paid on its return to OTIS & CO., 406 Broadway.

—February 22, 1862,
New York Herald

AN OPERA-GLASS, IN A BLACK MOROCCO CASE, was lost on Monday night at the Winter Garden by the young man who fainted. The finder will be suitably rewarded by returning it to No. 59 Bleecker st. or No. 630 Broadway, in the store.

—March 22, 1865,
New-York Times

LOST—CORAL AND GOLD bracelet—After the Matinee, on the 20th inst., P. M. between the Ladies' Drawing-Room at the Boston Theater and Beacon street via Washington and School streets. By leaving the same with JOSEPH PRATT, 164 State street, the finder will be suitably rewarded.

—January 23, 1866,
Boston Evening Transcript

LOST — THURSDAY EVENING, A POCKET-BOOK CONTAINING ball tickets, &c. The finder will be rewarded by returning the same to J. Helfman, 339 Broadway, upstairs.

—February 27, 1866,
New York Herald

the accumulation of material possessions, men and women rushed to fill their homes with beautiful things. Ornamental objects took on symbolic meaning: they defined one's financial standing and moral character within. During this Victorian period, manners were emphasized and a flurry of etiquette manuals advised men and women on virtually all aspects of daily living, including the proper attire for a day trip or an evening out on the town. Attending the right events and dressing the part became a collective middle-class priority.

Among women, this craving for fashionable goods paralleled a preoccupation with making crafts at home. Industrialization, with its labor-saving mechanisms, had begun to alleviate a number of household chores. Long used to hand-sewing entire wardrobes for their families, for example, mothers could now buy sewing machines (Isaac Singer introduced his to the market in 1851), or purchase ready-made clothing. Women suddenly contended with leisure time and the cultural pressure to spend it productively. Catharine Beecher, an advice writer in the nineteenth century, urged women to "have some *regular plan* for employment of your time, and in this plan have a chief reference to making home pleasant to your husband and children." Parlor crafts, or "fancywork," were widely sanctioned as useful ways to pass the hours after completing the daily round of domestic chores. "If one wanted to appear to be both busy and genteel," writes Beverly Gordon in *Making the American Home,* "it was especially appropriate to be seen doing ornamental or *fancy* work."

The popular magazines of the day offered practical tips and words of inspiration, expounding on the pleasures of embroidery, knitting, crocheting, leather work, shell art, lace work, beading, and other artistic endeavors. Those who showed talent were considered competent and well bred. It wasn't enough to own a cache of store-bought goods: women added artistic homemade touches whenever possible, stitching patterns, names, and mottos into bedding, bookmarks, screens, and any other plain surface that could showcase decorative work. A hand-sewn name, worked in the corner of a handkerchief, was a simple way to add virtue and meaning to an otherwise ordinary scrap of linen or cotton. These ornamental squares of fabric became popular gifts, given to close friends and family. Such fancywork paid homage to an earlier time, when the work of a needle was a daily necessity, not a pastime for the parlor.

> DROPPED—ON THE 7TH MARCH, AN EMBROIDERED Handkerchief, with Harriet worked in the corner. It was lost on the west side of Fifth avenue, between Eleventh and Twelfth streets The person who returns it to 100 West Fourteenth street will receive $1 reward, or more if required.
>
> —March 9, 1861, *New York Herald*

Another popular form of fancywork, also given away as sentimental offerings, was hair jewelry. Now curious relics from the past, these odd little pieces were once a rage. Hair, a symbol of life, was encased in lockets, rings, brooches, bracelets, pins, and other settings, as romantic tokens of love or mementos of grief. Hair jewelry had long commemorated deaths, engagements, weddings, acts of heroism, and other moments, both public and private. When Charles I died in 1649, for example, hair jewelry was made to commemorate his passing. More than two hundred years later, in 1861, when Queen Victoria lost her husband, Prince Albert, hair jewelry became part of her daily mourning attire. She coveted those pieces and helped turn the long tradition of hairwork into a widespread fashion statement.

Some women taught themselves the patient art of hairwork. A how-to book from 1876, complete with diagrams and step-by-step instructions, articulates the benefits of making these sentimental objects yourself: "The professional hair-manufacturers can doubtless perform this work more artistically, and bring it to a far higher degree of perfection than the mere amateur; but when we take into consideration the liability of having the hair of some other person substituted for that of our own cherished friend, or that careless hands have idly drawn through their fingers the tresses which it appears almost sacrilegious to have even looked upon with a cold glance, the thought is repugnant."

Still, some preferred to commission professional jewelers to custom design these one-of-a-kind relics. Strands were braided, plaited, coiled, twisted, knitted, and formed into long watch chains, bracelets, even chandelier-shaped earrings.

LOST—A HAIR BRACELET WITH A CLASP, also containing hair, lost on the way from West Twentieth street to Madison square, on the evening of the 17th of May. Of but little value to any but the owner, by whom it is highly prized, as containing the hair of a deceased child. The finder will be thanked or liberally rewarded, by leaving it at the office of WILSON & BROWN, 83 Beaver street, or at 99 West Twentieth Street.

—May 21, 1852, *New York Herald*

LOST—ON THE 30TH INST., NEAR TAYLOR'S SALOON, Broadway, a bead purse, containing a hair bracelet, and a small sum of money. The finder may retain the money, but will please send the bracelet, (it being a momento of a deceased friend,) to box 316 Post Office.

—February 1, 1855, *New York Herald*

Hair jewelry offered comfort during the Civil War years when more and more soldiers kissed their friends and families good-bye, leaving behind a lock or curl. An estimated 620,000 Americans never made it back home from that war; this gift may have memorialized one of those soldiers:

> LOST—On Main street, between the Spotswood House (ladies' entrance) and Col Wm Munford's room, over Mr Peterson's drug store, between the hours of 2 and 4 o'clock, on Saturday evening, the 26th inst, the farewell gift of a young soldier friend—his miniature likeness, on a Bristol board, and a silver-edged envelope, enclosing a lock of black hair. The gold framework of a breastpin, which was an inch long and not quite the same width, was also lost. The miniature was wrapped in a piece of white ruled paper. Around all the above-named articles was folded a small newspaper, either the Record or Register, which was carefully pinned at each end, forming thereby a square package of the size of a medium-sized envelope. Whoever may find the miniature and hair will please leave them in the hands of Capt Corkery, who will reward the finder and receive the best thanks of the lady who lost the package.
> mh 30—3t
>
> —March 31, 1864, *Daily Dispatch*
> (Richmond, Virginia)

By the end of the nineteenth century, hair jewelry lost its widespread appeal: the act of mourning, once displayed publicly through fashion, took on a more private role in people's lives. Instead, the photograph took over as the sentimental souvenir of the masses. In 1888, when George Eastman offered his compact, affordable Kodak camera for sale, preloaded with film and ready to shoot, he democratized the technology and changed the way people chose to remember their lives and their loved ones.

The hair relic, the opera glass, the embroidered handkerchief, tickets to an upcoming ball—these artifacts reveal how a growing number of Americans opted to spend their money and, for many, their newly acquired pockets of leisure time. Genteel objects stand out for their increased presence in Victorian-era papers—clearly these objects held a widespread social currency—but they appeared in the notice columns next to an odd assortment of everyday stuff. Indeed, part of the beauty of these lost and found postings is their serendipitous placement in the printed column. Nineteenth-century newspapers shoved missing and discovered belongings into one generic "Lost and Found" category. Tossed under the heading in no logical order, a missing sleeve button sits near an abandoned sailboat; seven thousand feet of pine board picked up at sea shares print space with four lost jeweled pins, one gentleman's shawl, and a veil. At times, less savory items could be found wedged between two elegantly refined ones. For all the tight controls that Victorian Americans imposed on their day-to-day lives, polite and thoughtful seating arrangements are refreshingly absent from the lost and found layout.

Lost and Found.

LOST—A GOLD SEAL RING, marked P., for which a suitable reward will be paid, upon returning it to 58 Franklin street.   3t¶   feb 28

LOST—On the Common, on the 23d ult , an ARTIFICIAL HAND. The finder will be suitably rewarded, on leaving it at the Transcript office.
3t¶   mh 1

LOST—On Sunday last between Boylston place and Newbury street, a gilt bound prayer book with gold clasp on which were initials, M. C. G. The finder will be suitably rewarded by leaving the same at 5 Boylston place.   3t¶   feb 27

—March 1, 1866, *Boston Evening Transcript*

THE SPOILS OF WAR

LOST—$10 REWARD. Lost, on the battle-field, near Gaines's Mill, an Army FIVE-SHOOTER. My name is engraved on the plate. The above reward will be paid for its delivery to me at camp near Blakey's Mill, or at my residence, on Marshall street, between 2d and 3d, in this city.

S. H. PENDLETON,
Jy 7---3t*   Lieut. Williamsburg Artillery.

—July 12, 1862, *Daily Dispatch* (Richmond, Virginia)

"Fairs, holidays, fair-weather Sundays, and especially the Christmas season, are the occasions when the greatest number of losses occur. Promotion in the news pages and a notation in the 'Found' group should remind all readers to advertise." This piece of advice came from Morton McDonald, the author of *Getting and Keeping Classified Advertising,* a manual published in 1936. Had McDonald written his book during the Civil War years, he might have added warfare to that list of potential high-loss occasions. Stressed out, sleep deprived, often on the move or under fire, soldiers had plenty of opportunities to get separated from their stuff. These ads, printed in a Richmond, Virginia newspaper, represent just a few of the items lost by Union and Confederate troops.

The matter-of-fact tone runs chillingly counter to the dramatic circumstances surrounding them. The location of the battlefield is tossed off casually, equivalent in print to Main Street or the market square. Drama may be absent from these postings, but not hope: soldiers who lost personal items during the Civil War banked heavily on the decency of the finders, including, in some cases, the moral makeup of the enemy.

strange red cow

FOUND—A BLANKET and OIL-CLOTH were dropped by a soldier Sunday evening during the rain. The owner can get them by applying at my house, corner of Grace and 1st streets.

COLEMAN WORTHAM

—June 18, 1862, *Daily Dispatch* (Richmond, Virginia)

LOST—Lost, at or within two miles of General Jackson's headquarters, on the 9th (Wednesday,) a Yankee KNAPSACK, letters "2d Reg V.V.M," on outside, containing many valuables to the owner—clothing, papers, &c. Particulars left with the publisher of the Dispatch. A reward of FIFTY DOLLARS will be given. BE HONEST.

—July 12, 1862, *Daily Dispatch* (Richmond, Virginia)

LOST OR STOLEN—A lot of FURLOUGHS for the wounded men of Banner Hospital, to which they feel they are entitled, and which they would be pleased to receive. Any information respecting them will be thankfully received by the PATIENTS of

BANNER HOSPITAL.

—August 2, 1862, *Daily Dispatch* (Richmond, Virginia)

SEVENTY-FIVE DOLLARS REWARD—Lost, on the battlefield at Coal Harbor, during the battle of the 27th ult., a pair of black patent-leather SADDLE-BAGS, containing one of Colt's latest improved six-shooting PISTOLS, with a fluted cylinder, a carved ivory handle, carrying a large ball, silver mounted, and engraved on the handle is the following inscription, as near as can be remembered: "Lieut. C.F. Tate, Aug. 1861." I value the Pistol chiefly on account of its associations, and will cheerfully pay the above reward for its delivery to me at Mrs. Davis's residence, on 4th street, between Clay and Leigh, or to Col. M. D. Graham, at the Exchange Hotel, no. 31. I will also pay the sum of fifteen dollars for the other contents of the Saddle-bags.

A.T. RAINEY
Col. of 1st Texas Regiment.

—August 2, 1862, *Daily Dispatch* (Richmond, Virginia)

FOUND—the officer who lost a cape in the battle below Drewry's Bluff on Monday, can recover it by applying at the Tredegar Works.

J.R. ANDERSON & CO

—May 21, 1864, *Daily Dispatch* (Richmond, Virginia)

LOST EN ROUTE

Some advertisers recorded exactly where they lost track of their things (or where they discovered someone else's) by retracing their steps and mapping their movements. Centuries later, such references to location can supply us with an informal primer on America's transportation history.

D ropt from the pommel of a side-saddle, on the 4th inst. about ten a clock, between the upper end of Arch-street and Charles Jenkins's ferry, A red leather trunk, with some wearing apparel therein ; said trunk was in a russet leather bag. Whoever will bring the same to the New-Printing-Office, shall have Twenty Shillings reward.

—October 5, 1752,
Pennsylvania Gazette

W AS found about two Weeks ago, a BRASS KETTLE, at the upper End of Front-street, supposed to be dropt out of a Waggon. The Owner thereof proving his Property, and paying Charges, may have it again, by applying to the Printers hereof.

—January 7, 1768,
Pennsylvania Gazette

In colonial times, roads were few and crudely carved, making horse-drawn transportation possible, just not very comfortable. Though water transportation often proved to be the preferred and quickest mode of transport, wagons, carts, and a modest number of carriages and stagecoaches were in use, and some contents fell accidentally from those vehicles.

Roads improved, cities grew in size in the nineteenth century, and new methods of public transportation—the steamboat, the railroad, the omnibus, the horse-drawn streetcar, the electric trolley—joined old ones on the road and in the water. Then, as now, every journey generated the possibility of forgetting one's belongings.

strange red cow

$10 REWARD—Will be paid immediately for a basket of clean clothing left on the dock at Whitehall by mistake, by a person going down in the steamboat Staten Islander, at 7 o'clock on Saturday evening, 6th inst. The above reward and no questions asked, will be paid by leaving said basket at 93 Washington st.

—June 10, 1840,
New York Sun

$15 REWARD—LOST, ON THE HUDSON RIVER Railroad, in the quarter to 5 o'clock train from New York, a set of teeth on a gold plate. They were dropped out of the window on the right hand side of the way, supposed between the Tarrytown and Sing Sing stations, or at a short distance this side of Tarrytown. The finder will be rewarded on leaving them with the ticket master at Sing Sing, or by directing a letter to 268 Ninth street, New York.

—April 4, 1855,
New York Herald

L EFT—LAST EVENING, IN ONE OF THE RED BIRD stages, a Book entitled "Jane Eyre." By returning to 42 Pine Street, room No. 7, a liberal reward will be paid.

—January 25, 1862,
New York Herald

L OST — ON THURSDAY MORNING, 11TH INST., IN AN Amity street stage, a Package of Silk, wrapped in a newspaper. The bundle also contained a sample of silk, wound on a spool or piece of paper. By returning the same to the owner, with Gordon, Bowdoin & Manen, 299½ Broadway, upstairs, the party will confer a great favor and receive a suitable reward.

—September 13, 1862,
New York Herald

As the cost of carriage production decreased in the last quarter of the century, more Americans could afford to trade their simple wagon for a more comfortable buggy with springs. For city dwellers, a private carriage could be hired from a nearby livery stable, much like a taxi or car service today.

lost and found

LOST—ON SUNDAY MORN-ING, IN PASSING OUT TO the Park from Twenty-seventh street via Madison avenue to Forty-first street, and from thence via Fifth avenue, a leather Phaeton* half cushion. The finder will be suitably rewarded by leaving it at 227 Fifth avenue.

—March 14, 1865,
New York Herald

LOST—ON SUNDAY, COR-NER OF BROADWAY AND Twelfth Street, a Leather Curtain from a carriage. The finder will receive a suitable reward on leaving it at Mr. Nicols' stable, 25 East Twelfth street.

—October 16, 1865,
New York Herald

LOST—On Saturday afternoon, 18th inst., on the road between Salem and Swampscott, a carriage WHIP, gold-mounted, and marked "J.C." A *liberal* reward will be paid to any one leaving the same at the corner of Franklin and Baker streets, Lynn.

—August 20, 1866, *Boston Evening Transcript*

Lost. BETWEEN Federal St and Boston and Maine Depot, a gold plated Carriage door handle. The finder will be rewarded by leaving it at No. 89 Federal Street.

—February 18, 1875, *Portland Daily Advertiser* (Maine)

Lost—ON SUNDAY AFTER-NOON, a carriage Lamp. A liberal reward will be paid if returned to 238 West Twenty-seventh street.

—March 10, 1875, *New York Herald*

* *Phaeton* describes any number of horse-drawn carriages with four wheels.

In September of 1897, the first electric subway cars were introduced to Boston. New York unveiled its underground track in 1904; Philadelphia, in 1907. With crowds of commuters taking advantage of these lines, the lost and found pile accrued daily. In those early years of underground transit, the piles were manageable enough to itemize, and then make public to commuters by way of the classifieds.

LOST AND FOUND.

FOUND.

Found.—July 31 and August 1—Interborough Rapid Transit Co.s lines. Ask Lost and Found Department, 39 Greenwich st.:—

SECOND AVENUE ELEVATED.

Hat; Three Satchels; Irons; Purse; Bill Case; Shoe; Knife; Shawl; Vest; Package Handkerchiefs; Baseball Glove; Shirt; File and Chisel; Pair Shoes; Overalls; Bag; Umbrella.

THIRD AVENUE ELEVATED.

Belt; Overalls; Bags; Three Packages Aprons, Books; Truss; Two Shirts; Cuffs; Lock; Coat; Burlap; Box Candy; Pair Shoes; Toy; Keys; Purse; Bag; Package Coffee; Bathing Suit; Pair Gloves; Key, &c.; Bottle Liquid; Pair Trousers; Package Laundry; Photographs; Pocketbook; Screen; Comb; Two Pieces Wood; Eight Hats; Four Umbrellas.

SIXTH AVENUE ELEVATED.

Hats; Bottle Oil; Box Checkers; Two Bathing Suits; Package Laundry; Box Powder; Bottle Liquid; Envelope; Pair Gloves; Cap; Waist; Pair Glasses; Scarfpin; Underwear; Safe; Roll Papers; Legal Papers; Sweater; Package Papers; Overalls; Rule; Music Case; Shoe; Two Umbrellas.

NINTH AVENUE ELEVATED.

Two Coats; Pocketbook; Package Collars; Two Packages Papers; Keys; Ring; Three Purses; Letter; Overalls; Apron; Jumper; Rubber Cape, &c.; Pin; Gloves; Book; Fan; Shoes; Hat; One Umbrella.

SUBWAY.

Hat; Roll Wire; Two Boxes Cigars; Four Purses; Book; Check; Railroad Ticket, &c.; Wallet; Glasses; Pin; Shirt; Books; Bag; Pair Gloves; Pocketbook; Railroad Commutation Ticket; Pair Spectacles; Photos; Bonnett; Box of Gum; Pair Shoes; Pair Rubbers; Buckle; Bathing Suit; Suit Case; Coat; Five Hats; One Cane; Eight Umbrellas.

—August 3, 1909, *New York Herald*

lost and found

A Curious Moment in Classified History

Keys seem determined to part ways with their owners. In 1811, residents in this Rhode Island community instituted a system to better cope with the pattern.

LOST KEYS.

BY request of a number of the inhabitants of this town and vicinity, the Clerk of the Market has consented to receive KEYS from those who have or may find them, and deliver them to the owners free from any expense, on a proper description being given.

☞ If this notice is properly attended to, it will be a great convenience, and save much expense.

—January 11, 1811, *Rhode-Island American, and General Advertiser*

It's a logical premise, a numbers game: the likelihood of loss increases in spaces inhabited routinely. And how people navigate a landscape—the paths they take and the vehicles that take them there—delineates some of those spaces. Cars replaced carriages in the twentieth century, and the plane introduced a new method of travel, carrying commuters each day across distances that once took weeks or months to traverse by horse or by boat. References to these modern-day modes of transit slip unconsciously into twenty-first-century classifieds. Originally meant to locate lost and found objects in time and space, they inadvertently record how we manage to get around today.

lost: yoga mat

Reply to: anon@craigslist.org
Date: 2004-09-12, 1:39PM CDT
Purple yoga mat fell off my scooter somewhere between UT and
183/Anderson Mills. . . .
this is in or around central/north Austin
—September 12, 2004, *www.craigslist.com*
(Austin, Texas)

Lost surf board!!!

Reply to: anon@craigslist.org
Date: 2004-10-23, 10:22AM PDT
OK I am a dumbass. I left this board on my roof and it came off at this
intersection. It is 6'6 Mystic shaped by John Moore. Help!!!! Reward.
This is in or around Great Hwy and Skyline.
—October 23, 2004, *www.craigslist.com*
(San Francisco, California)

Found: One jetta hubcap

Reply to: anon@craigslist.org
Date: 2005-02-13, 8:41PM EST
To the woman driving a Green Jetta at the corner of Hope st. and
Doyle ave. at approx 1:15pm on Sunday 2/13. As you raced to beat the
light you lost your rear driver's side hubcap. I found it because it rolled
through the intersection and hit my car. Please pick it up along with the
bill for filling the scratch.
this is in or around Hope/Doyle
—February 13, 2005, *www.craigslist.com*
(Providence, Rhode Island)

Bestial Wanderlust

> ### Stop my Pig !
>
> ABSCONDED from his lodgings a male pig seven or eight weeks old, of the Newbury white breed. Whoever may have taken him into custody, or seen him in his wanderings, and will give information thereof at this office; will be compensated. He was last seen at full speed taking an air line for Vassalborough the place of his nativity.
>
> —September 7, 1832, *Kennebec Journal* (Maine)

Belongings lifted from lost and found notices, dusted off and classified themselves, could fill a museum of material culture. But inanimate objects tell just part of the story: a procession of missing and discovered animals also turned up in print. Vintage hues once described the "mouse-colored she asses," "strawberry spotted cows," "fawn colored pugs," and "milk-white Arabian horses" that wandered off, then surfaced soon after in the local newspaper. Cows named Betsy and Peggy and Nellie all went missing, as did sows "heavy with swine," even large flocks of sheep. In the notice columns, practical objects and precious keepsakes were stacked next

> #### Advertisement.
>
> STray'd on *Monday* laft, a fmall red Cow, with a yellow and black ftrip't Lift about her horns, a little Tet on one of her Tets. Whoever fhall find faid Cow, & her bring to *John Campbel* Poft-mafter of *Bofton*, fhall be well rewarded.
>
> —October 2–9, 1704, *Boston News-Letter*

strange red cow

to sorely missed family pets and farm animals that turned up on someone else's property.

This "small red Cow" was the first stray to show up: she arrived in the *Boston News-Letter* in the fall of 1704, just a few months after those two iron anvils disappeared from Mr. Shippen's Wharf. As he often did in those early years, John Campbell, the publisher of that paper, offered his services as the middleman.

Farm animals have been wandering off in America ever since the colonists first introduced themselves and their animals to the New World. The settlers who dropped anchor off America's East Coast found a landscape rich with wildlife. Early records describe woods crowded with deer, pheasant, and wild turkeys, fields full of migrating ducks and flocks of pigeons, and waters teeming with an inexhaustible supply of fish—all home to the Native Americans who had thrived off the land's natural resources for thousands of years. There were plenty of wild animals running free, but the tradition of raising farm animals in captivity was not a part of Native American culture. The settlers brought that tradition with them, along with a supply of livestock from their homeland. It's difficult to confirm which animals, if any, joined European settlers on their journey to Jamestown, Virginia, in 1607. Two years later, though, Captain John Smith noted the presence of pigs, chickens, horses, goats, and sheep, and by 1617, 128 cattle, 88 goats, and countless swine were observed in that colony. It took almost four years for Plymouth to boast of any cattle: in 1624, Edward Winslow transported "three heifers and a bull, the first beginning of any cattle of that kind in the land."

This livestock population played a major role in transforming the region's cultural and physical landscape. The colonists believed that the influx of domesticated animals was good and necessary for the proper development of the country, and they imposed those views on their native neighbors, insisting that they, too, raise livestock. Clergyman Roger Williams, founder of Rhode Island colony, didn't mince words when he encouraged the Indians to shift from "Barbarism to Civilitie, in forsaking their filthy nakednes, in keeping some kind of Cattell." But for many Native Americans, keeping farm animals was an impractical headache at best and at worst, a cultural and spiritual violation. It was impossible to venture out on a hunting trip when a herd needed care and management, and swine foraged for the same nuts and berries, depleting the local food supply. Aside from the dog—which the Native Americans had widely domesticated—animals raised in captivity conflicted with the Native American's long-established spiritual relationship to the natural world, where beasts had the same rights to the land as humans, and an animal was considered property only after it was killed.

If these conflicting cultural perspectives weren't enough to alienate the natives from the newcomers, the habits of the livestock divided them daily. In early New England, colonists fenced in their crops, but permitted their animals to often wander at large in nearby woods or along public ways. Cows and swine frequently strayed into any field they could find, devouring unprotected crops. Those same animals ignorantly disturbed traps set by the natives. If a roaming animal was injured by one of those traps, or accidentally or intentionally killed while wandering, it was the Native American who suffered the fine. This was a disorienting and unjust rule for those long used to freely hunting the range of wildlife they encountered in the woods. Public records show that Native Americans routinely issued complaints to colonial authorities about these pesky strays, and that colonists themselves issued complaints against each other. Throughout the eighteenth century, inserts placed in the notice columns confirm that bes-

STRAY'D, about two Months ago, from the Northern Liberties of this City, a small bay Mare, branded I W on the near Shoulder and Buttock. She being but little and barefootted, cannot be supposed to be gone far; therefore if any of the Town-Boys find her and bring her to the Subscriber, they shall, for their Trouble, have the Liberty to ride her when they please; from

Philad. June 17. 1742. William Franklin.

—June 17, 1742, *Pennsylvania Gazette*

STrayed out of the pasture of Adam Cantz, last July, sixteen sheep, nine are slit in the near ear, some with both ears cut off, some with one ear cut off, one with a bell, and one ear cut off, three are black, and one not right black. Whoever takes up said sheep, and brings them to Ralph Sarver, at the Rising sun, or secures them, so that the owner may have them again, shall have Fifteen shillings reward, and reasonable charges, paid by ⊕ RALPH SARVER.

—January 2, 1750, *Pennsylvania Gazette*

TAKEN UP at Black-creek, about eight miles above Fort-Argyle, on Ogechee river, by Israel Bird, A BAY HORSE, about 13 and a half hands high, with a bell on; has a small star in his forehead, branded on the near shoulder thus ⊕ O, or like three o's joining, and on the off shoulder I W. The owner must prove his property before

Ogechee, May ELISHA BUTLER.

—May 31, 1764, *Georgia Gazette*

NOTICE is hereby given, That I have two large black stray Horses in my Custody; each of them has a Bell on, one is three Years old, and branded on the mounting Cheek thus, 2. The other is about twelve Years old, and branded on the mounting Thigh thus, 3. ——— Whoever claims said Horses, may have them again, proving their Property, and paying the Expences, to

THOMAS ROBESON, Junior, living in Bladen-County.

—July 10, 1765, *North-Carolina Gazette; And Wilmington Weekly Post-Boy* tial wanderlust was an ongoing source of grief and tension in the colonies.

Legislation was adopted to control the trespassing. The laws varied from town to town, from colony to colony, and from year to year depending on the local animal population and their most aggravating offenses. Proper identification generally helped maintain order. To keep track of strays, colonists were legally required to earmark or brand their animals. Earmarks of various combinations (nicks, slits, croppings, holes, etc.) differentiated one animal from the next, as did initials or patterns branded squarely on a horn or a thigh. Registered markings became an administrative family heirloom, inherited by each generation much like a piece of property.

Some owners didn't bother to brand their animals, and without those man-made markings to reference, missing livestock could only be identified by their natural distinguishing features. It was more difficult to reclaim an unmarked stray; they were easy targets for thieves and convenient additions to another farm's inventory.

STRAY'D away from the Subscriber, living in New-Haven, some Time in June last, A young brown Mare, two Years old past, paces and trots, no Brand, and is not dockt. Whoever will take her up, or inform me where she is, so that she may be had again, shall have a Dollar reward and all necessary Charges, paid by me
NATHAN MANSFIELD.

—September 20, 1765,
Connecticut Gazette

strange red cow

Fences also helped keep roaming beasts in check. Initially, in communities where animals grazed at large, fencing was the responsibility of anyone with private property to protect. Fences were erected around gardens, orchards, and fields full of crops to keep out stray animals. In New England, official inspectors—"fence viewers," they were called—made sure these enclosures met town standards. By the late 1700s, however, many towns had assigned the fencing responsibility to the owners of livestock instead, requiring them to formally enclose their animals or risk paying fines.

But in spite of these and other legislative efforts, animals still managed to wreak considerable havoc. While a farmer worried about an animal he couldn't account for, someone else, perhaps not too far away, was dealing with that very same stray. Finding an animal on your property was no doubt an inconvenience: there was the cost of the newspaper notice (if the finder chose to insert one, though, if the rightful owner stepped forward, that sum was usually reimbursed), the temporary care of the animal, and the reparations of any crop or property damage caused by the stray. Some finders were less tolerant than others.

> CAME to my plantation on the Beaver Dams, Screven county, in October, 1799, A large BRINDLED COW, marked in one ear with an under bit and upper bit, had loft the other ear, and had no perceptible brands. She broke into my enclofure, and did me fo much damage as to oblige me to kill her. Any perfon having a claim for faid cow is defired to come forward.
>
> THOMAS LOVETT.
>
> —March 27, 1800, *Georgia Gazette*

lost and found

In 1800, when Thomas Lovett placed his ad in the *Georgia Gazette*, 5.3 million people lived in America. Then, the Louisiana Purchase of 1803, considered one of the most expansive land deals in history, kicked off a century of dramatic expansion; some 830,000 square miles of land, bought at roughly four cents per acre, practically doubled the size of the country. Industrialization, westward expansion, and the ongoing process of urbanization transformed America's economic and physical landscape. By 1900, the population of the United States had multiplied to 76 million. More people meant more animals, and even with an increasing number of fences in place, stray livestock continued to play a prominent role in the lost and found columns of the newspapers.

Even in dense urban centers, livestock roamed the cityscapes. New York City, the country's biggest metropolis—roughly half a million residents lived there in 1850—was particularly hard hit by the problem. In 1842, Charles Dickens rode through the city recording the scene of the day: the "glittering shops," "lively whirl of carriages," and "various parasols" all caught his attention; so did the squalor of the Five Points slum and the city's population of free-roaming swine.

> **$5** REWARD—Strayed or stolen from the premises of Michael Farrell, 106 Madison st, on Thursday, 19th inst, a large white sow, remarkable for shape, lame in one of the forward feet, half gone in young, long tail, generally curled. Any person returning said hog, or giving information where she may be found, will have the above reward with the thanks of the owner.
>
> —May 23, 1842, *New York Sun*

strange red cow

STRAYED OR STOLEN

FROM my premises, in Big Cane, on the 4th of last February, a dapple gray stallion, about 5 years old next spring, 14 hands high, heavy mane and tail, heavy built and fat, no mark or brand visible, right fore foot hoof just grown off with foot evil. A liberal reward will be paid for his delivery to the undersigned, or for such information as may lead to his recovery.
E. B. CARTER.
Big Cane, St. Landry, March 7 1863—14—2t

—March 7, 1863, *Opelousas Courier* (Louisiana)

NOTICE.—An estray SOW has been hankering around my lot for three or four days, and I have confined her in my lot. She is spotted, with a crop off each ear. Any person having lost such a hog, can find her at my house.— I wish they would come, pay expenses of advertisement, and carry her away. H. A. TERRELL, near corner of Coots and St. Stephen streets. de 31—3t*

—December 31, 1864, *Daily Dispatch* (Richmond, Virginia)

FOUND.

A STRAY COW HAS BEEN visiting my garden every night for the past two weeks, and I have taken her up and put her in my stable, where the owner can get her on proving property and paying charges. The cow is white and brown, with some black on the head; has a brand like an L on the left thigh. SARRAILLE PETER,
no5-3* Near Bay View Park, San Bruno Road.

—November 7, 1867, *Daily Alta California*

LOST, STRAYED, &c.

LOST COW.—Strayed from Henrico county Court-House, a medium sized white and red COW; answers to the name of "Nellie;" young and in good order, with left horn damaged from contact with locomotive; is marked in both ears, a slit in the right and a scollop cut from the under part of the left (I think.) A reward of $5 will be paid for her return.
je 24—3t* THOS. A. STAPLES.

—June 24, 1862, *Daily Dispatch* (Richmond, Virginia)

Local city markets supplied meat and poultry, but at a high price, so working-class households often raised their own animals to defray those costs. With space at a premium, many ran free, generating chaos and filth in the streets. Butcheries and piggeries added to the fray by letting their animals run wild. Dickens warned visitors to the city to watch out for the "ugly brutes": "Two portly sows are trotting up behind this carriage, and a select party of half-a-dozen gentlemen-hogs have just now turned the corner." And he described their nightly ritual after a long day of scavenging: "Every pig knows where he lives, much better than anybody could tell him. At this hour, just as evening is closing in, you will see them roaming towards bed by scores, eating their way to the last."

The same year that Dickens wrote those lines, an editorial in the *Daily Tribune* claimed that the ten thousand roaming pigs were significantly contributing to the city's sanitation problems (though pigs helped with garbage pick-up, they left behind piles of waste).

> $2 Reward—Strayed or stolen about the 10th inst, a Berkshire boar; his color was black, mixed with white hair. His left ear cut off, and the right cut a little. The finder will receive the above reward and the thanks of the owner by leaving the same or giving information where he may be found, at 39 Broome st.
>
> J. LOCKWOOD.
>
> —February 22, 1842, *New York Sun*

The city struggled to control the pig population for years, periodically running large numbers of swine uptown, past 86th Street. It wasn't until 1860 that large-scale hog pens were shut down and the bulk of the city's pigs were successfully pushed northward to the less developed neighborhoods, relieving the crowded downtown grid of the long-standing headache. Pigs could still be found scavenging in the streets, no doubt, but in far fewer numbers.

The pig population, as troublesome as it was, made up just one strand of New York City's stray livestock problem. Goats and sheep were among the other farm animals that populated the metropolis; and slaughterhouses, over two hundred of them within city limits in 1850, further complicated the picture. Cattle were routinely herded through city neighborhoods, adding to the congestion and, at times, injuring pedestrians en route. In 1853, the city's Common Council finally outlawed daytime cattle drives south of 42nd Street, but the issue of trespassing cattle still lingered—on the streets and in the notice columns.

SUPPOSED TO HAVE GOT OUT OF THE YARD OF the slaughter house 193 Orchard street, two red cattle, tarred on the right side. The finder will be rewarded by leaving word with John Reeves, corner of Laurens and Houston streets, or at L. Cook's grocery, corner of Orchard and Houston streets.

—February 2, 1855,
New York Herald

$10 REWARD WILL BE PAID FOR INFORMATION which will lead to the recovery of an ox which was stolen or strayed in the early part of this week from the droveyard corner of Forty-fourth street and Madison Avenue; or he may possibly have jumped into the North river from pier 21. Apply to John Hogan, 95 East Forty-eighth street.

—August 3, 1862,
New York Herald

The horse, an indispensable tool of daily nineteenth-century living, couldn't help but contribute to the chaos. In *A History of Public Health in New York City*, John Duffy sketches the scene: "To recreate the atmosphere of old New York, one has to visualize a good sized city in which horses supplied the chief motive

A Curious Moment in Classified History

For the return of his odd-looking hen, this advertiser was willing to pay fifty dollars—twice as much as many posters offered for stray horses at the time.

$50 REWARD.—STOLEN, ON WEDNESDAY (17TH) evening, between 9 and 10 o'clock, a curiously deformed Hen, without a beak, and head shaped somewhat like a monkey; highly valued as a curiosity. The above reward will be paid by returning the hen to No. 234 William street, N. Y.

—May 19, 1865, *New York Herald*

power for transporting men and goods. They hauled the garbage and night soil, delivered both milk and water, and were omnipresent in the streets." In mid-century, an estimated 22,500 horses dragged public vehicles up and down city streets and an unrecorded number towed private carriages and carts.

As the American economy became more industrial and less agriculturally dependent, the frequency of stray livestock notices dwindled. Cars eventually replaced horse-drawn transportation, farms receded from the urban landscape, and bestial wanderlust became less of a pressing public concern. No longer a nuisance of everyday life, the sight of a trespassing barnyard animal making its way through the cityscape today has all the makings of an entertaining human interest story. Such was the case when William Grimes, a writer for the *New York Times,* spotted a black chicken in his Queens, New York, backyard in the winter of 2001. The food critic adopted the hen and relished her weekly output of fine eggs. But when she mysteriously moved on just a

STRAYED OR STOLEN— FROM ATLANTIC STREET, third door above Powers, a black horse about 16½ hands high, white star on his forehead, two white hind feet, very heavy mane and tail, to a light rockaway wagon, made by Ezra Marsh, Newark, N.J., a blanket covering the horse marked E., also a robe under the back seat. The finder of the above will be liberally rewarded by returning him (he is Logan stock) at JAMES MORRIS' stable, Liberty Street, Brooklyn.

—May 19, 1857,
New York Herald

STRAYED OR STOLEN—A BROWN HORSE, WITH farm Wagon, painted red and loaded with family stores; when last seen was at the foot of Dey street, at 2 o'clock P.M., 19th inst., in care of a man slightly under the influence of liquor. A liberal reward will be paid to any person giving information of the above. Apply to John S. Young, Chief of Detectives, 300 Mulberry street, or to E. Martin, 125 and 127 Hudson street.

—January 21, 1865,
New York Herald

STRAYED OR STOLEN—A WHITE SPOTTED SMALL Horse, a spavin* on hind right leg, with a small light Fish Wagon, painted red, a common box attached, from Fulton Market, on Friday morning. The finder will receive $10 reward by returning it to Frederick Nawstedt, Centre Hill, Hudson City.

—August 8, 1865,
New York Herald

LOST—ON THE 27TH INST., ABOUT 8 P.M., A BAY Horse, with halter and blanket. Whoever will return the same to the Knickerbocker Ice Company's stable, 17 Leonard street, will be suitably rewarded.
H. H. NELSON

—March 1, 1866,
New York Herald

STRAYED OR STOLEN— FROM THE STABLE OF Henry Vantine, during the fire on Thursday evening last, at 413 East Tenth street, a Black Mare, 15½ hands high, 12 years old, tail square on end. A suitable reward will be paid on delivery or for information concerning her.

—November 10, 1867,
New York Herald

---

* Spavin is a disease that causes a horse's hock joint to swell.

few months later, he chose not to post a reward notice for her: "I envisioned a line down the block, one reward seeker after another with an identical black chicken tucked under his arm." Instead, he wrote about that short-lived "rural chapter" in the Food section of his newspaper, then published a book on the subject, *My Fine Feathered Friend*. "If anyone happens to see a fat black hen," Grimes announced to his readers, "tell her this for me: There's a light in the window and a warm nest at the base of the pine tree."

BITCH, BEST FRIEND, BABY

The first two European canines to settle permanently in New England, a mastiff and a spaniel, arrived with the *Mayflower* in 1620. By 1635, colonial authorities had already instituted dog-ownership laws for such canine offenses as "killing sheep and swine, biting horses and cattle, spoiling fish and entering Meeting Houses during ser-vice." Postings for lost and found dogs and other pets appeared in eighteenth-century newspapers, although with less frequency than ads for stray livestock. Dogs held a number of essential jobs in the colonies: hunters, livestock managers, exterminators, security guards, among them. Their widespread practical contribution helped shape the owner-animal relationship. Surely, colonists cared about their pets, but early notices typically communicate little emotion, often striking the same matter-of-fact tone as their stray livestock counterparts.

The tenor of the pet notice began to shift in the nineteenth century, as cultural interest in pet keeping intensified. Victorian culture promoted acts of charity, of treating others with kindness.

The middle-class home provided the ideal environment to model this concept of benevolence, a hands-on classroom where a child could learn to treat a pet properly. Mrs. Child, a well-known writer of how-to books, included this advice in her 1831 manual, *The Mother's Book:* "Kindness towards animals is of great importance. Children should be encouraged in pitying their distress; and if guilty of any violent treatment toward them, they should see that you are grieved and displeased at such conduct." Such emphasis on caretaking naturally generated close bonds with the animals. Emotional distance, a hallmark of the eighteenth-century lost-pet ad, showed signs of narrowing.

WAS loft, on Friday Morning, from Charles Jenkins's Tavern, in Market ftreet, a large black and white Hound; is chiefly white, and has a large round black Spot on one of his Sides, another on his Loins, and another on the Side of his Neck, intermixed with red Hairs; his Head and Ears are of a redifh Colour, with a Blaze down his Face; a very deep tongued Hound. Whoever will bring him to the faid Tavern, or, if concealed, give fuch Information, that the Owner may get him again, fhall have Twenty Shillings Reward.

—March 28, 1765, *Pennsylvania Gazette*

LOST, *A black and white Bitch*, with a remarkably large white fpot in her face; fhe is very far gone with young, and anfwers to the name of *Fly*. Whoever delivers the faid Bitch to me, near the Independent Church, fhall receive *Five Dollars* reward. H. PERONNEAU.

—June 11, 1778, *South-Carolina and American General Gazette*

In addition to the dog, the cat was also regularly adopted in Victorian America, as was the cage-bird. Cats were actively employed as mousers and ratters, keeping disease-carrying rodents at bay. Cage-birds were coveted for the vibrant colors and sounds they ushered into the home. Before the invention of the phonograph in 1877, Americans had just a few musical options available to them: singing, playing an instrument, or listening to the sweet notes of a songbird. Birds lacking musical talent could fill a quiet home with aviary chatter.

For owners in search of other pet options, titles like the *Book of Household Pets and How to Manage Them,* printed in 1866, led the way. In addition to canines, the resource manual counts pigeons, fancy poultry, possums, fish, rabbits, white mice, guinea pigs, squirrels, and raccoons among its list of rewarding pets to own. Squirrels are described as "elegant in form and cheerful in disposition," even capable of showing great affection. "Some exhibit excessive fondness for those who keep them, and will come and nestle in their bosoms and play all kinds of engaging tricks." To prospective raccoon owners, the book offered this warning: "a very amusing companion; but never gets over his fondness for chickens. He will have to be supplied with green corn and vegetables, but will help himself to tidbits from the poultry-yard, if not watched."

LOST—From 11 Oliver st, on Saturday the 1st of August, a Canary bird, with green wings, green tail, green top knot, and body yellow; being a particular favorite, the lady will give one equally as good and her sincere thanks to whoever may return it.

—August 11, 1840,
New York Sun

$16 REWARD—Escaped from the lower part of Broadway, a beautiful GREEN PARROT with a red head; speaks Spanish like a native. Any person bringing him to this office will be handsomely rewarded.

—August 19, 1851,
Daily Alta California

ESCAPED, from No. 1 Cambridge street, yesterday afternoon, a SMALL BIRD of the parrot species, called "Lorita"; color green, and every way resembling a parrot. Whoever will return the same shall be suitably rewarded, and receive the thanks of the owner.

—March 27, 1858,
Boston Evening Transcript

$2 REWARD—A CAT LOST, ABOUT TWO MONTHS ago, from the corner of Prince and Greene streets, a white Cat, with black tail, a little black on his head, over one eye, a few spots on his back, and a little spot at the end of his nose. That reward for his recovery or such information as would lead to it, at 120½ Greene street.

—April 5, 1861,
New York Herald

CAT LOST—$5 REWARD. A Malta and White CAT, about one year old, marked by white feet and by pink ribbons in her ears. Whoever will return her to No. 8 Asylum street, shall receive the above reward.

—June 25, 1866,
Boston Evening Transcript

FOUND ON THIRD STREET, ON FRIDAY last, a dead Canary Bird, prepared for stuffing. Owner will apply at 272 S. Third St.

—September 17, 1866,
Public Ledger (Philadelphia)

Pet keeping flourished in the 1800s, along with a growing market of supplies designed to make the relationship between owner and animal more satisfying. The first commercial pet stores in America were bird stores, which opened their doors in the 1840s. In 1895, James Spratt is believed to have launched the first commercial dog food in America. Until kitty litter was invented in 1947, a box of old newspapers or ashes was the best an indoor cat could hope for. Once kitty litter became widely marketed and available, the cat became a more desirable companion, now outnumbering dogs as the most popular pet in the United States.

The 1948 ad placed by Mr. and Mrs. Dooley, opposite, captures the spirit of the modern-day pet notice: earnest and heartbroken. It is a theme repeated daily in the classified section of local newspapers and on websites that function as bureaus for missing animals. The emotional distance between human and animal, once built into the eighteenth-century lost-pet notice, has all but vanished. More pets now live in America than people: two hundred and ninety million humans claim to own three hundred and

> On Friday, December 19, Smoky,
> a tan and gray tiger cat, part
> Persian, nine years old, strayed
> from home, 32 Carnation Road. Mr.
> and Mrs. M. Dooley say they miss
> their cat terribly. They will pay a
> reward to anyone who finds Smoky.
> —January 15, 1948, *Levittown Eagle*
> (New York)

seventy-seven million pets. Major brand names long associated with human products—Lands' End, Ralph Lauren, and Harley-Davidson, among them—are creating lines that promise cleaner, happier, healthier animals. All the marketing seems to be working; according to the American Pet Products Manufacturers Association, Americans spent more than thirty-four billion dollars on their animals in 2004. Gifts included pressed rawhide greeting cards, leather biker gear, kosher snacks, salon-quality shampoo, and nail polish.

As our emotional—and financial—investments grow, we invent new technological systems and gadgets to keep our pets near. Electronic fences draw invisible boundaries; implanted microchips store essential contact information; global positioning systems track down those gone astray. The growing market for these high-tech systems reminds us that our domesticated animals will always have the urge to roam. Accidentally leave open a gate, a window, or a cage, and an animal will likely sneak out and explore. In neighborhoods across America, there are pets out wandering right now; some of them, no doubt, will meet in the classifieds.

ORANGE CAT STILL MISSING since 8-11-04 (concord / pleasant hill / martinez)
Reply to: derrogative@hotmail.com
Date: 2004-10-24, 10:38AM PDT
Escaped on aug 11th this year from our house around the Port Chicago/Olivera rd area, and is still missing. He is over a year old, yellow eyes, and has mostly red/orange/golden fur..not stripes but swirls. He is short haired, very soft to the touch like silk. He is a fairly large cat, un-neutered and was not wearing a collar and is not microchipped. The most distinct thing about him is the tan freckle on his pink little nose. When this cat meows, he really meows. Kind of sounds like a crying baby. His name is Ozzy, if you think you have seen him or know any information that would help us find him please email me. I am desperately hoping that he is found or comes home, we miss him sooo much.. we don't have any children so he is our kid.

I have pictures of him, just ask in the email and i'll be happy to send you them, thanks.

—October 24, 2004, *www.craigslist.com* (San Francisco, California)

LOST: Male Black & Tan chuiahua/pom/min. pinscher mix
Reply to: anon@craigslist.org
Date: 2005-03-04, 3:15PM PST
Just heard about posting on craigslist. We lost our Lil black and tan chuiahua/pom mix on News Year eve or day. We were away and came back the next day, January 1, 2005 and he was missing. He's buddies with our pit bull and they hang out together, my pit was still home he was gone. Either someone took him or he got lost. My house is gated and he must have crawled under when the fireworks were going off and someone found him and now he can't get back home. Please he's our baby and my daughters and me miss him. He was wearing a lil red coat and weighs only 4 1/2 lbs.

—March 4, 2005, *www.craigslist.com* (Sacramento, California)

strange red cow

COIN RETURN

As customs, trends, and societal mores change, so, too, do the content and tone of the lost and found advertisement. Perhaps the best way to trace this evolution is not by studying ads for one object unique to a particular era, but by tracking the development of something that has never gone out of style in America: money. Coins came over with the English in the early seventeenth century, but in short supply. Without a monetary system in place, early settlers depended heavily on barter. Animal pelts, nails, tobacco, and other commodities were exchanged in place of coins. Introduced to the newcomers by the Native Americans, wampum—cylindrical beads fashioned out of shells and strung together in patterns—proved to be a popular form of exchange.

Since the English government forbade the colonies from minting their own money but failed to provide an ample supply, colonists relied heavily on foreign coins for years. At trading ports, Spanish, English, Portuguese, and other metal currencies passed hands. Then, in defiance of English law, a mint was established in Boston in 1652. There the colonies' first coins were struck: crude pieces of silver known as New England coinage.

Paper money appeared in 1690, again in Massachusetts, when bills were generated to pay soldiers returning from a military expedition in Canada. Other colonies followed step, the last being Virginia: paper money wasn't issued in that state until 1755. On any given day, a colonist's pocketbook might have contained any number of foreign or domestic coins, bills of credit issued by several different colonies, or notes of hand (I.O.U.'s), much of which still followed the system of pounds, shillings, and pence. Exchange rates fluctuated from colony to colony, which made financial transactions on the road rather complicated.

Lost on the Ninth Instant, a Leather Pocket-book, containing about Eleven Pounds in Paper Money, Pennsylvania Currency, Nineteen Shillings and Ninepence, Virginia Currency, and Seven Shillings and Fourpence, North Carolina Currency; as also several Promissary Notes, particularly one for Seven Pounds Fifteen Shillings, Carolina Money. and one for Two Pounds One Shilling and Sixpence, Pennsylvania Money ; likewise a Journal of the Road from Lancaster to North Carolina. Whoever has found said Pocketbook, and brings it to the Harp and Crown, in Third-street, Philadelphia, shall have Fifteen Shillings Reward, if the Money is brought with it, but if the Papers alone, Five Shillings, paid by JAMES GAMBLE.

—October 12, 1758,
Pennsylvania Gazette

DROPT, on Monday last, at the City Vendue-House, or betwixt that and the Church Burying-Ground, an old green Purse, in which was a HALF JOHANNES.* Whoever has found it, and will bring it to the New Printing-Office, opposite the Jersey Market, shall be rewarded for their Honesty.

—August 25, 1768,
Pennsylvania Gazette

---

* The Johannes (also known as the "Joe") originated in Portugal and was one of many coins that made its way from foreign trading ports to the colonies. Like paper money, figuring out the value of any one coin in any given colony was confusing. Tables published in almanacs outlined the various rates of exchange. In 1759, *Father Abraham's Almanack* valued a Half Johannes at 2 pounds, 17 shillings, and six pence in Philadelphia; the same coin was worth 3 pounds, 3 shillings in New York.

In 1775, the Continental Congress authorized the printing of Continental currency, America's first federally printed money. These Continentals were meant to help finance the revolution, but were backed not by silver or gold, but by much anticipated and not-yet-collected tax revenues. Individual states were meant to do that collecting, but that plan collapsed. Rampant counterfeiting, especially by the British, further deflated the value of Continental currency, which depreciated dramatically over the next few years. By 1780, the bills were worth just a fraction of their original value.

LOST on the Eighteenth or nineteenth inst. between Shrewsbury and Hubbardston Sixty-nine Pounds some Shillings raped up in a clean piece of paper, chiefly CONTINENTAL MONEY; there was Four THIRTY DOLLAR BILLS in said Money. Whoever will return the above Money to me the Subscriber shall have TEN DOLLARS Reward.
OLIVER FAIRBANKS.
Hubbardston, November 21, 1777.

—December 19, 1777, *Massachusetts Spy or, American Oracle of Liberty*

On April 2, 1792, President George Washington signed into law the establishment of the United States Mint in Philadelphia, the country's temporary capital at the time. By that summer, the mint was producing official United States coins. For cash supply, the country relied on private banks to generate their own notes. With no federal oversight dictating either the design or size of the bills, banknotes lacked uniformity. Then, in 1861, the government, in need of money to pay for the Civil War, issued "Demand" notes, also called "green-backs" for their color. In 1863, Abraham Lincoln pushed for a national banking system and Congress passed the National Banking Act. National notes eventually replaced state chartered bank bills.

> LOST—ON TUESDAY, ON BROADWAY OR IN A FIFTH avenue stage, going down town, a morocco Portmonnaie, containing over fifty dollars in national currency. The finder will be suitably rewarded by leaving the same at the piano warerooms, 684 Broadway.
>
> —February 14, 1866, *New York Herald*

A dramatic development in America's currency occurred fifty years later, in 1913, with the creation of the Federal Reserve System, the nation's central bank. In an effort to oversee regional banking activity, the government established Federal Reserve branches in twelve different cities (where they remain today). Though the design of the bills has evolved, we still carry around Federal Reserve notes in our wallets today.

> LOST—On Sunday evening last, about half a mile east of the Ten Mile House, on the Mormon Tavern road, a purse containing about one thousand dollars in dust.* I think the purse was marked "Bradley & Clay." The finder will be liberally rewarded by leaving it at this office, or at Keith & Davenport's Store, on J street, between 4th and 5th.
>
> —September 2, 1850, *Sacramento Transcript* (California)
>
> ---
>
> * In late January 1848, gold was discovered along the American River in California. During the rush that followed, gold dust became an acceptable and popular form of monetary exchange in western mining communities.

strange red cow

The changing face of money, coupled with its widespread use and appeal, makes it a particularly interesting possession to track in the classifieds: anyone can spend it, everyone understands its value, and there is no easy way to prove true ownership.

LOST, A POOR SERVANT GIRL, WHO WAS GOING to send her wages, saved since a long time, to her poor old mother in Ireland, lost the money ($25 in gold, and the remainder in bills and silver) yesterday morning at 6½ o'clock, in going from the corner of Columbia and State streets, Brooklyn, to 22 Exchange place, in New York. The honest finder is requested to deliver the money back to the very poor girl, at 42 Willow place, Brooklyn, or 22 Exchange place, basement, New York.

—April 25, 1855, *New York Herald*

$25 REWARD—LOST, ON TUESDAY EVENING, IN THE Sixth avenue, $51, every dollar the owner possessed in the world; with Wedding Ring of deceased wife. The finder may divide with the loser and leave the money and get reward of H.B. Melville, jeweller, 76 Bleeker st.

—June 1, 1865, *New York Herald*

LOST—ON SUNDAY EVENING, JULY 14, ABOUT NINE o'clock, in crossing the Hamilton ferry, by a poor widow having four orphans to support, a Pocketbook containing $81, in greenbacks and some pennies. Any person finding it will be rewarded and have the blessing of the poor widow and orphans by leaving it with the ferrymaster at the gate or with Mrs. Hughes, at 23 State street, Brooklyn, upper floor, front room.

—July 16, 1867, *New York Herald*

$100 Reward—Lost, a pocketbook, on Front street, between the south side of Madison and the alley north of Monroe street. A reward of $100 will be given to the finder on returning the same to the owner at 55½ Jefferson street. No questions will be asked. The loser is a poor man, and has lost the accumulations of several years of hard labor. The book contained $285 and a little small change.

L. CAMPODONICO.

—June 16, 1875,
Daily Memphis Avalanche

In the 1700 and 1800s, and well into the 1900s, newspapers routinely ran ads for *found* currency; sometimes several appeared in the same column on the same day. Finders of cash, bags of coins, even piles of "bankable" gold dust, often went to great lengths to reunite those sums, no matter how large or small, with their rightful owners. Returning any object is an act of solid citizenship, but those who made the effort to return found currency seem particularly upstanding.

FOUND.—THE . LADY WHO, ABOUT FOUR WEEKS ago, lost some change in the store 185 Bowery, will please call and receive the same, as it has been found.

—January 14, 1865, *New York Herald*

Found.

BETWEEN Nevada and Mill Creek, on Tuesday, June 19th, a purse containing $1,152, in bankable dust. The owner can have it by proving property and paying charges. 96-1t J. H. COWAN. Mill Creek.

—June 23, 1866, *Montana Post*

FOUND ON MAIN ST.

A quantity of money which the owner can have without the hope of fee or reward. Simply state when you lost it; now much; kind, etc. Don't call but address WELL. G. SINGHI, 185 Broadway, Rockland, Me., and if yours I will see you get it at once. 45-5

—November 21, 1893, *Rockland Courier Gazette* (Maine)

strange red cow

A Curious Moment in Classified History

We have no idea what motivated this advertiser, who apparently waited years before stepping forward to return this money.

> **F**OUND, FOUR DOLLARS, WHILE LEAVING THE CARS at Paterson, in the summer of 1845. The loser (or agent) is requested to identity, in some respect, and receive the amount with interest. Address, pre-paid, I Found, Lower Post Office, N. Y. city.

—March 30, 1849, *New York Herald*

Open up a newspaper or scan online classified sites today and you may find ads for found money. They are out there, to be sure, but the climate has definitely changed. Those who lost money seem braced for disappointment. One recent online ad for a missing wallet captures the tone of our current-day cynicism:

Brown leather wallet
Reply to: anon@craigslist.org
Date: 2004-02-16, 6:13PM EST
Sure, it's a huge long shot, but why not?
I lost my wallet (dark brown leather, tri-fold) at the Solomon Pond Mall on Friday the 13th. Probably in Theater 9 of the movie theatre there. If you found it and stripped it of the money and gift cards, that's fine. But I'd really like my social security card back. Please email me with any info. Thanks.
—February 16, 2004, *www.craigslist.com* (Boston, Massachusetts)

Porter

Swan

Bell

Pig

Rofe

Turk

CHAPTER 2

The Runaway
Slave Notice

STRAY'D away from Samuel Strudwick, Efq; at Wilmington; A bright bay Horfe, about 12 and ½ Hands high, a Star in his Forehead, with a Roach Mane & Switch Tail; has no other Brand than a fmall burnt Speck on one of his Buttocks.——Whoever brings the faid Horfe, and delivers him to Mr. James Walker, fhall have a Reward of Twenty Shillings Proclamation Money.

RAN away from the faid Strudwick, a Negroe Wench, named Betty —Twenty Shillings, and all Expences, paid by Samuel Strudwick, for lodging her in Gaol.
—July 10, 1765, *North-Carolina Gazette; And Wilmington Weekly Post-Boy*

The language and format of the stray-livestock notice bears a striking and unsettling resemblance to another category of postings: ads for runaway slaves. Slavery marked the cultural, economic, and political underpinnings of American life for more than two and a half centuries. The system of slavery was integral to the life and livelihood of Americans in the North and the South. Reflecting the general mindset, postings for lost farm animals and fugitive slaves can appear graphically interchangeable. To the farmer or planter, both were commodities, to be bought and sold and put to work involuntarily. In his memoir, first published in 1845, abolitionist and statesman Frederick Douglass addressed the blurring of human and nonhuman boundaries in the eye and mind of the slaveholder: "Men and women, old and young, married and single, were ranked with horses, sheep, and swine. There were horses and men, cattle and women, pigs and children, all holding the same rank in the scale of being, and were all subjected to the same narrow examination. Silvery-headed age and sprightly youth, maids and matrons, had to undergo the same indelicate inspection."

In 1619, colonist John Rolfe of Jamestown, Virginia, husband to Pocahontas, bought twenty Africans from the captain of a Dutch warship. Considered the first permanent Africans to settle in colonial America, they likely held the same status as white indentured servants. By 1800, there were close to one million slaves living in the United States. On the eve of the Civil War, the country's slave population had more than quadrupled. The runaway notice helps fill in the stark outline of those sweeping statistics, offering thumbnail sketches for at least a portion of those who tried to break free.

Not all owners posted ads for their runaways, however. "A count of fugitive advertisements during any time period will reveal the *minimum* number of fugitive escapes during that period," writes Daniel Meaders, in *Dead or Alive*. Some slaves were apprehended or killed before making it very far; others returned on their own. Money was also a deciding factor in determining whether to run an ad. An owner was responsible for paying the initial price of the posting and the reward specified if the fugitive was caught, not to mention the cost of jail fees or return transportation—all of which could add up to a financial liability, especially if the fugitive had gained sufficient ground. But with these postings as testimony, plenty of advertisers did think it worthwhile to make announcements in the local newspaper. Some rushed to place notices while others waited weeks, months, even years. We don't know exactly how many slaves made escape attempts, but the large volume of runaway advertisements in the newspaper, along with the labyrinth of legislation drafted to control their flight, gives some shape to the pattern.

COLD PROFILES

Some ads were penned loosely, others with astounding and disturbing detail. The finer the description, the more likely a passerby or jail warden could have positively identified a runaway. The name of the fugitive was typically noted. Stripping a human being's identity began with the renaming process. Owners chose a variety of names for their slaves; origins ranged from Anglo-Saxon (Violet, Jack, Harry) to Latin and Greek (Caesar, Pompey, Neptune) to biblical (Moses, Sarah, Abel). There were those who protested this practice by preserving their "country" names and choosing culturally significant namesakes for their newborns. "Particularly prominent was the African practice of naming children after important days, events, and places," explains Ira Berlin, author of *Many Thousands Gone:* "Thus on December 25, 1743, 'Christmas' was born on one South Carolina plantation, taking the name of a holiday that derived from Europe but maintaining the traditional African form of naming." Of course, a runaway could have changed his or her name, creating a new identity en route, and that practice was written into the ads themselves.

Some owners included a reference to gender and took a guess at age, if the precise number of years was not known. Overall, there were more runaway notices for males than females and younger slaves were more inclined to flee than older ones. This can be attributed,

---

Eight Dollars Reward.
RAN AWAY from the subscriber, living in Paxton township, Dauphin county, about 6 miles from Harrisburg, on Friday, the 19th instant, a Negro BOY, named SAM, 17 years of age, 5 feet 9 or 10 inches high, well made, has very large feet, large featured, and thick lips, much pitted with the small-pox; had on when he went away, a brown coloured hunting-shirt, under jacket with strings to it, and trowsers of the same, a pair of coarse tow trowsers, and a linen shirt. It is probable he will change his name and clothes. Whoever takes up said Negro, and secures him in any jail, so that his master may get him again, shall have the above reward, and reasonable charges.
BENJAMIN DUNCAN.
December 26, 1794

—December 31, 1794, *Pennsylvania Gazette*

FIFTEEN DOLLARS REWARD—
Runaway from Major William Ball's in Chesterfield county, near Manchester, on Monday the 22nd of May last, a very likely small Negro fellow named JAMES, but I understand he has changed his name, and calls himself HENRY, he has an impediment in his speech, is about 20 years old, supposed to be about 5 feet 7 or 8 inches high, he is very well acquainted in Richmond, Manchester and Petersburg, is a very cunning and artful fellow, and I expect will endeavor to get on board of some vessel to go by water. I therefore forwarn all Masters of vessels and others from harboring of him, or carrying him off at their peril. Whoever will deliver the said fellow to Major Ball near Manchester or to the subscriber near Chesterfield court house, shall receive the above reward.
EZEKIEL JACKSON.
JUNE 27.

—June 27, 1809, *Richmond Enquirer*

---

strange red cow

at least in part, to the fact that the slave trade placed a higher premium on young, healthy men. But other factors influenced the gender and age imbalance of the average runaway. Life as a fugitive demanded great physical endurance: the weather could be cruel, the food supply scarce, and the journey to safe harbor long and treacherous, if safe harbor was ever reached at all. The chances of success and survival were decreased for women with babies on their hips or elderly slaves; they appear less frequently in ads than young, fit males, but they do, indeed, turn up.

Advertisers made note of skin color, height, weight, texture and style of hair (in some cases, wig), condition of teeth or gums, shape of eyebrows, size of cheeks, nose, lips, hands, feet, pockmarks,

---

WILLIAMSBURG, May 5, 1773. RUN away from the Subscriber, on *Saturday* the 1st Instant, a Negro Woman named JUDITH, who carried her Child with her, a little Girl at the Breast, about twelve Months old. I bought her but the Day before, at the Sale of the Slaves of Mr. *Austin Smith of Middlesex*, in this Town, and having her so short a Time in my Possession, I am not able to give a particular Description of her, but think she is middling tall and slender, not very black, appears to be between thirty and thirty five Years of Age, and I have been since told she is with Child. I expect, if she is not already gone back to *Middlesex*, she will soon endeavour to return to her former Master (Mr. *Smith*) or some of his Neighbours. Whoever secures her so that I may get her again shall have FOUR DOLLARS Reward if she is taken in *Williamsburg*, SIX DOLLARS if taken in *Middlesex*, and delivered to Mr. *Hugh Walker* there, and so in Proportion to the Distance of any Place she may be apprehended at. I shall take it as a Favour of Mr. *Smith* if she returns to him to give Directions for securing and conveying her to me in *Norfolk*, and any Expense attending the same shall be thankfully repaid by

JOHN MACLEAN.
—May 6, 1773, *Virginia Gazette*

---

the runaway slave notice

dimples, moles, freckles. No detail, it seems, was considered too small or insignificant to mention.

Posters sometimes remembered a slave's exact height but typically characterized body type in more generic terms: "thin made," "squat made," "very well made," "rather spare made," "clumsy made," "raw boned," etc. Skin colors were described as "coal black," "jet black," "very black," "deep black," "handsome black," "pretty black," "not very black," "of dark color, but cannot be said to be black," "of black cast, but not the very blackest," "dark griff color," "a copper color," "olive colour," "rather of a tawney than proper black colour," "dark brown or gingerbread color," and so on.

> West Pennsborough township, Cumberland county, August 22, 1770. RUN away from the subscriber, about the 26th of July last, a Negroe man, named ABEL, of middle age and size, a smith by trade, has a little halt as he walks, and turns out his toes, had, sometime ago, a large wart under his waistband, and I think a bit hath been taken out of his ear. Whoever secures said Negroe in any goal so that the owner may get him again, shall have FOUR DOLLARS reward, and reasonable charges, paid by me
>
> THOMAS BUTLER.
>
> —August 30, 1770, *Pennsylvania Gazette*

Close attention was also paid to missing limbs, fingers, or toes, poorly healed broken bones, twisted ankles, swollen joints or lips, scratches, scars—any obvious or intimate irregularities. Ritualistic markings, evidence of African heritage, were noted, as were wounds and health conditions: the mark of smallpox, traces of frostbite, sunburn, or the symptoms of a bad cough.

At times, advertisers explained the origins of a slave's injury. In a notice posted in August of 1803, Roger Farrell, the manager of Lawrence Lewis's plantation in Virginia, wrote that the runaway, Peter, "has a large scar on one of his legs, occasioned by the cut of a scythe last harvest." In 1769, Mary Myer, a female advertiser in South Carolina, made a point of mentioning how her young slave, Molly, contracted marks on her stomach.

the runaway slave notice

> Philadelphia, June 17, 1745. RUN away from the Sloop Sparrow, lately arrived from Barbados, Joseph Perry Commander, a Negro Man, named John; he was born in Dominica, and speaks French, but very little English; he is a very ill featured Fellow, and has been much cut in his Back by often Whipping; his Cloathing was only a Frock and Trowsers. Whoever brings him to John Yeats, Merchant in Philadelphia, shall have Twenty Shillings Reward, and reasonable Charges, paid by John Yeats.
>
> —June 20, 1745, *Pennsylvania Gazette*

Though certain injuries may have been the result of work-related or childhood accidents, many slave owners and overseers committed heinous acts of physical abuse.

That a slave was last seen wearing an iron neck collar or an iron leg clog was not considered out of the ordinary. Owners routinely shackled these iron devices onto the limbs and necks of repeat or potential runaways; in some instances, slaves were shackled to each other. Owners and overseers shared this information in the same anesthetized tone used to describe the color of a runaway's teeth or the make or condition of his clothing.

> RUN away, last Thursday, from Philip Syng, of this city, silversmith, a Negroe man, named Cato, about 20 years old, a short, well-set fellow, and speaks good *English:* Had on when he went away two jackets, the uppermost a dark blue halfthick, lined with red flannel, the other a light blue homespun flannel, without lining, ozenbrigs shirt, old leather breeches, yarn stockings, old shoes, and an old beaver hat. When he went away he had irons on his legs, and about his neck, but probably has cut them off, as he has done several times before on the like occasion; he generally skulks around this City. Whoever brings him home, shall have *Twenty Shillings* reward, and reasonable charges, paid by
>
> PHILIP SYNG.
>
> —May 5, 1748, *Pennsylvania Gazette*

strange red cow

RAN away the 15th of July last, from Crump's Neck, a Plantation belonging to the Hon. William Byrd, Esq; in the County of Hanover, a whitish Mulatto Man Slave, called Dick: He is about 24 Years old, and of a middle Size, with the Letter R branded on his right Cheek, and a large Scar on the Calf of his right Leg. Whoever shall take up the said Mulatto, and bring him to the Subscriber at the Falls of James River, be he Free Man or Slave, shall have Three Pistoles Reward.* Witness my Hand

Nelson Anderson.

—August 11–18, 1738,
Virginia Gazette

RUN away from Samuel Read, living near the new Forge, the 9th inst. September, A likely Negroe Man, named Peter, about 5 feet 8 Inches high; Had on when he went away, a gray Jacket, also a red Stuff† ditto, old coarse Trowsers, soaked with Apple-juice, and old Shoes. He is much given to laughing, and has some Marks on his Back and Belly with the Horse-whip. Whoever takes up and secures said Negroe, so that his Master may have him again at the new Forge, shall receive Forty Shillings Reward, and reasonable Charges, paid by me

SAMUEL READ.

—September 29, 1763,
Pennsylvania Gazette

RUN AWAY from the plantation of John Bowman, Esq. at Skidaway the 9th June last, a NEGROE WENCH, named Esther, branded on the breast J. Bowman, but perhaps the brand may be blotched; she is about 37 years old. Any person delivering her to the Warden of the Work-House shall receive a reward of 10 s. and all reasonable charges; and whoever will convict any person of harbouring her shall have 30 s. reward.

EDWARD SIMMONS

—July 13, 1774, *Georgia Gazette*

---

* The pistole was a common name for a Spanish gold coin, which circulated widely in the colonies.
† A textile used to make clothing, typically a wool or worsted material.

the runaway slave notice

Kingstown, Queen Ann's County, September 10, 1759 RUN AWAY the 8th of this Instant, a Negroe Man, named Caesar, he has both his Legs cut off, and walks on his Knees, may pretend that he was Cook of a Vessel, as he has been much used on board of Ships; he was seen by New-Castle on Saturday last. Whoever secures the said Negroe in any Goal or Work-house, shall receive Twenty Shillings Reward, paid by me SARAH MASSEY.

N.B. He has been a Ferry man at Chester Town, Queen Ann's County, for many Years.

—September 20, 1759, *Pennsylvania Gazette*

Ten Dollars Reward. RAN away from the subscriber (living in Loudon county, Virginia) about the 7th of October, 1805, a Negro Woman by the name of CHARLOTTE, a low and well set wench, about the age of 24 years, has large white and full eyes and very thick lips, with a mouth of vast capacity; but, what I suppose to be the most remarkable, and by which she may be easily known, is a large bare place on the back part of her head. I deem it unnecessary to mention her clothing, as the length of time which she has been absent has given her an opportunity of changing them. I will give the above reward to any person or persons, who will either deliver her to me, or confine her in any goal, so that I get her again, and all reasonable charges I will also pay. *Nicholas Grimes*, near Mr. Wm. Hummer's Tavern, January 27.

—January 27, 1806, *Alexandria Daily Advertiser* (Virginia)

Nansemond, June 20, 1768. RUN away from the subscriber some time in *April* 1767, a new Negro man named TOM, belonging to the proprietors of the *Dismal Swamp*. He is about 5 feet 6 inches high, has his country marks (that is, four on each of his cheeks.) Any person that apprehends the said fellow, so that I may get him, shall have three pounds reward, paid by

JOHN WASHINGTON

—June 23, 1768, *Virginia Gazette*

> TWENTY DOLLARS REWARD will be paid for the return or for information resulting in the return to me, of my cook HARRIET, who ran off to Richmond, August 6. She is a bright, thin-breasted, tall, sneaking mulatto. She can read, is a Methodist, sings very loud, and is disposed to argue. Was severely whipped August 1st. Supposed to have on a black skirt and red body, colored straw bonnet and blue ribbons—Shows fine teeth when spoken to. I bought her of Dr. Dorsey, of Maryland. Age 35.
>
> H.P. TAYLOR.
>
> —September 26, 1862, *Daily Dispatch* (Richmond, Virginia)

Although more than a few advertisers chose *not* to list a runaway's clothes—anticipating that the slave probably had ample "opportunity of changing them"—many did think it useful to report that information. The details can be dizzying: type of fabric, size of buttons, make of shoe buckles, color of handkerchiefs, condition of boots or hats or coats. The same efforts that owners took to meticulously chronicle their runaways' facial features or body blemishes were channeled into itemizing their

> FIVE POUNDS REWARD. RUN away from the Subscriber, in the upper End of *Caroline* County, the last Week in *May*, two Negro Men, ABRAHAM and CAESAR, the former is about 6 Feet 3 or 4 Inces high, is a strong well made Fellow, a Shoemaker by Trade, is a fine Plantation Hand, has had a Sore upon one of his Shin Bones nearly as large as a Dollar, and I expect the Scar is still fresh. *Caesar* is a Planter, stoops a little in his Shoulders, is an outlandish Negro, and his Temples are full of grey Hairs. I purchased both of the said Slaves last *October* from Col. *Philip Rootes* of *King* and *Queen* County, where I have Reason to believe they are gone. Whoever will take up and deliver the said Negroes to me shall receive the above Reward, or FIFTY SHILLINGS for either of them.
>
> ANTHONY THORNTON, Junior.
>
> —June 27, 1777, *Virginia Gazette*

the runaway slave notice

R AN away from one of the plantations of Richard Beresford, Esq; about three months since, a very sensible young negro fellow, called Salisbury, well known in St. Thomas's parish: He is short and well sett, has lost one of his fore-teeth, and had an iron clog on each leg at the time of going away. Any person delivering him to the warden of the work-house, in Charles-Town, or any of Mr. Beresford's overseers, shall receive a reward of FIVE POUNDS currency from the subscriber; who is in want of a quantity of SASSAFRAS-ROOT, clear of the stumps of the trees, to be delivered in Charles-Town, or will take it at any landing upon a rea-sonable allowance for the freight.

WILLIAM LOGAN

—January 25–Feb 1, 1768, *South Carolina Gazette*

apparel. When fugitives carried off a supply of stolen clothing, clues to those garments were mentioned as well. Runaways escaped in all seasons of the year, though in the north, it was easier to survive outside during the warmer months; still, some made their break in the dead of winter when

T HREE POUNDS *Reward.* RUN away from the subscriber, living near Canawingo Creek, Little Britain Township, Lancaster County, on Friday, the 15th of January, a Mulattoe woman, about 18 or 19 years of age, she calls herself HANNAH CAMBEL, is a bold well tongued hussy, of a whitish cast, very much freckled in the face, has a brown spot on one of her lit-tle fingers, and commonly wears her hair tied; had on, when she went away, a light coloured lincey jacket and petticoat, and it is supposed she had other clothes, she wore white stockings, with blue clocks, high heeled shoes, and it is thought she will dress herself in mens clothes. Whoever takes up said wench, and brings her home to her master, or secures her in any of his Majesty's goals, so as he may get her again, shall have the above reward, and reasonable charges, paid by

MOSES DAVISON.

—February 24, 1773, *Pennsylvania Gazette*

extra layers of clothing were needed to fend off freezing temperatures and frostbite. Carrying along several changes of clothing also helped camouflage identity.

In addition to clothing, some runaways took objects or animals with them. Horses and boats were brought along for transportation, dogs presumably for protection. Items that could aid a fugitive in flight or could help generate income along the way—food, guns, swords, canes, money, tools, bedding, musical instruments, etc.—also left plantations and farms with runaways.

Along with these physical descriptions of what a slave looked like or wore or carried off are all sorts of behavioral observations. Unlike newspaper notices advertising the sale of slaves, also prevalent in eighteenth- and nineteenth-century newspapers, runaway ads did not profit from slick salesmanship. Owners advertising a slave for sale focused primarily on attributes, characteristics that emphasized a slave's monetary worth to an owner.

> TO BE SOLD, On the 30th day of this instant, A MULATTO SLAVE, near six feet high, well made, a compleat hand for a ship carpenter, as he can saw with any kind of saw, use an adze, broadaxe, or auger, is a special hand at getting timber for shipping, blocking off and hewing, has worked some time at the business: He can also reap and mow, both with cradle and naked scythe, in doing which, few, if any, can excel him. Enquire of Mr. WILLIAM THARP, Merchant, in Front street, near Walnut-street, Philadelphia.
>
> —October 20, 1778, *Pennsylvania Packet*

But a master searching for a runaway was apt to give a broader picture, pointing out a slave's strengths and weaknesses, talents and perceived thoughts. Thus, an owner might have taken note of a fugitive's

the runaway slave notice

R UN AWAY from the subscriber, a NEGROE MAN, named JASPER, about 30 years of age, five feet two inches high, has his country marks down his temples, has been used to a boat, talks good English, and is very well known about town; he took away with him a canoe. Whoever takes up said Negro, and commits him to the jail in Savannah, or delivers him to me at Abercorn, shall have ten shillings reward.

ANDREW LAMBERT

—August 18, 1763, *Georgia Gazette*

L OUISA, March 18, 1776. RUN away from the Subscriber on the 16th Instant a likely Negro Fellow named JACOB, who is about 5 feet 5 or 6 Inches high, 30 Years old, square and well made, is very black, and has a down Look; had on, and took with him, a coarse blue Cloth great Coat, a fine brown mixed coloured Broad-cloth Body Coat, double-breasted scarlet Cloth Waistcoat, a Pair of very good Buckskin Breeches, knit Yarn Stockings, very good Hat and Shoes, and also several Shirts of white and brown Linen, and some Money. He was born in *Pennsylvania*, bred a Farmer, pretends to great skill in Farriery, speaks in the *Scotch-Irish* Dialect, and in Conversation frequently uses the Words *moreover* and *likewise;* and as he can read and write, will probably forge a Pass. Whoever takes up said Slave, and secures him so that his Master may get him again, shall have 40 s. if taken in *Louisa, Albemarle,* or *Orange;* if in any other County in the Colony 5 l. and if taken out of the Colony 10 l.* paid by
DAVID HOOPS.

—March 30, 1776, *Virginia Gazette*

---

* Geographic distance often informed the amount of the reward offered, increasing exponentially if the slave was discovered far from his owner: 1 pound (£) equaled 20 shillings (s.) and 1 shilling equaled 12 pence (d.)—based on the individual currency of each colony, not sterling. Thus, the reward promised to the finder who discovered Jacob outside the colony of Virginia (£10) was five times more than the amount set aside for an individual who "secured" him locally (40 s.).

strange red cow

gift for music, language proficiency, affinity for alcohol, professional accomplishments, reading and computation ability or inability. A slave adept at reading and writing posed a particular threat to an owner: literate fugitives could forge the documentation necessary to leave the plantation. Slaves traveling outside the jurisdiction of their owners were required to carry a pass or ticket along with them; without this documentary proof, they were treated as runaways and dealt with according to law. Those caught supplying illiterate runaways with forged passes or tickets also faced punishment.

For all the specifics packed so neatly into these ads, not all the information presented can be trusted. In profiling their slaves, owners or overseers expressed subjective opinions about the way a fugitive was prone to act ("very turbulent in her temper," "can frame a smooth story from rough materials," "has a particular wink, or leer, with his eyes when talking"). But how a person behaved in bondage was unquestionably different from how he interacted in the free world. A runaway known for his stuttering, "a stoppage in his speech," might have exhibited that impediment only when psychologically stressed. Likewise, an individual described as surly, disobedient, or capable of violent behavior likely revealed those temperaments in response to a hateful owner or overseer.

The runaway slave notice is a complicated document; it contains a wealth of information, but it is written about slaves and not by them. Each posting requires close analysis. "One must challenge, contest and raise questions about every ad, and use caution to guard against being misled," warns Daniel Meaders in *Dead or Alive.* "Ads were mug shots, not portraits," reminds the historian Kirsten Sword. We can gather useful findings from these classifieds (the names given to slaves, their musical or linguistic or professional talents, the clothing they once wore or carried off with them), but other observations are far less reliable.

THE WILL OF THE CAPTURED

Runaway ads tell the first part of the story and "Picked Up" or "Now in the Goal" announcements contain at least a fraction of the follow-up. Many runaway slaves were seized en route and then secured in a local jail. There, the warden or sheriff on duty posted his own ad in the paper in search of the runaway's master. In such cases, we are given a glimpse into the fate of a fugitive. A slave named Caesar ran away from John Hall's Maryland plantation on November 16, 1762. On December 23, Hall posted a runaway notice in the *Pennsylvania Gazette;* right below his ad, a jail warden posted a notice for Hall:

> RUn-away on the 16th of November last, from the Subscriber, living on Saffafras River, Cæcil County, Maryland, A Negroe Man, named Cæfar, of a middle Stature: Had on, and took with him, A Felt hat, a blue Broadcloth lappelled Coat, with Metal Buttons, a green Cloth Vest, brown Cloth Breeches, white Linen Shirt, white Yarn Hofe, and new Shoes, tied with Strings, and small Nails drove round the Heels and Soals. He pretends to understand something of the tight Cooper's Business. Whoever takes up faid Negroe, and gives Notice thereof to his Master, or secures him, so as he may be had again, shall have a Reward of Six Dollars, and reafonable Charges paid, if brought Home, by
> ¶   JOHN HALL.
>
> New-Castle, December 2, 1762.
> NOW in the Goal of this County, A Negroe Fellow, calls himself Cæfar, fays he belongs to John Hall, Efq; in Cæcil County, Maryland; his Master is hereby defired to come, in four Weeks after this Date, pay Charges, and take him away, otherwise he will be fold for the fame, by
> *   ALEXANDER HARVEY, Goaler.
> N. B.   He is a Cooper by Trade.

But a "Picked Up" or "Now in the Goal" notice didn't guarantee the return of the runaway. The location of capture may have been far from the owner's property, and the advertisement published in a paper rarely or never read by the master. If the slaveholder didn't come forward within a designated period of time, the fugitive was typically sold to a new owner at auction.

The punishment was severe for anyone convicted of hiding a fugitive or encouraging a slave to escape. As could be expected, compensation was awarded to those who reported fugitives to local authorities. In Virginia in 1705, for example, 200 pounds of tobacco could be earned for "taking up" a slave at least ten miles from the owner's property; if less than ten miles, but more than five, that amount dropped to 100 pounds of tobacco. On top of what the local laws doled out, a runaway notice usually offered an additional reward. Compensation varied depending on the slave's worth to the master, and the amount printed in the first advertisement could have doubled or tripled or even increased tenfold in subsequent postings.

On June 15, 1832, a notice in the *New Orleans Bee* offered a twenty-five-dollar reward for the return of two slaves named Neck and Benn. The posting ran in that newspaper for three months without success. By the September 15 issue, the advertiser had significantly increased the reward:

ONE HUNDRED DOLLARS REWARD.
RANAWAY from the other side of the river, on Saturday last, the two Mulatto boys named NECK AND BENN. NECK is about 5 feet 6 inches, aged about 19 years. BEN is about 5 feet 10 inches, aged about 21 years. They have been seen near the Rail Road. Whoever will lodge the said slaves in the jail of this city, will receive the above reward on application to this office.

—September 15, 1832, *New Orleans Bee*

the runaway slave notice

Captured slaves, reclaimed by their owners, often endured barbaric punishment back at the plantation or farm. Laws were put into place to try to standardize such punishment, and fines were imposed on slaveholders who neglected to heed them. Legislation varied over time and place. South Carolina passed a particularly cruel set of laws in 1712, outlining the complicated consequences that runaways (sixteen years or older) were meant to suffer if declared missing for a stipulated number of days: as many as forty lashes for the first offense; the letter *R* branded on the cheek for the second attempt; up to forty lashes and one ear cut off after the third try for freedom; fourth-time male offenders were castrated; fourth-time female offenders were whipped, branded with an *R* on the left cheek, and the left ear was dismembered. Caught for the fifth time, a fugitive was formally tried and if found guilty, part of his leg was cut off. Execution was a legal alternative.

Although most advertisers wanted their slaves returned to them in good health, some advertisers wished violent harm on their runaways.

RUN away from the subscriber, a Negro man named MANN, about 5 feet 6 inches high; he has a slit in one of his ears, gives very sensible answers, and is about 50 years old. He is outlawed from his threatening to burn my houses. If any person will deliver me his head, severed from his body, they shall receive 10 l. current money: If taken alive and delivered, 40 s. besides what the law allows.

JOHN SMITH

N.B He is supposed to be lurking about Col. *Corbin's* quarters, in *King &*
Queen.

—February 4, 1768, *Virginia Gazette*

strange red cow

Such unconscionable violence was a warning to all slaves. But the risk of incalculable pain, even the threat of death, did not discourage many thousands from plotting escapes and carrying them out. Men, women, and children, suffering from broken limbs, "lame" legs, even legs cut off at the knees, tried to make the break from bondage. Women with children in their arms, their breasts "full of suck," took to the road in the name of freedom. Determined slaves "made a practice out of running away." No amount of punishment could have convinced some of them to stop trying.

WE HOLD THESE TRUTHS TO BE SELF-EVIDENT

American newspapers are a registry, albeit an incomplete one, for runaways and the advertisers who looked for them. Occasionally, a name we all recognize surfaces in the records. Out of the first twelve presidents of the United States, nine owned slaves. In 1799, the last year of his life, President George Washington managed more than three hundred slaves at Mount Vernon. Determined to set his slaves free, he outlined his emancipation plan clearly in his will, the only Founding Father to do so: "Upon the decease of my wife, it is my Will & desire that all the Slaves which I hold in my *own right,* shall receive their freedom." Nearly four decades earlier, in the summer of 1761, Washington's motive was quite different. When Peros, Jack, Neptune, and Cupid fled his plantation one Sunday in August, he composed a lengthy ad and posted it in the *Maryland Gazette.*

Washington's slaves chose to escape on Sunday for a reason. In *An Imperfect God,* Henry Wiencek explains: "Three of them disappeared wearing Sunday clothes, such as the 'dark colour'd Cloth

Fairfax County *(Virginia) August* 11, 1761.

RAN away from a Plantation of the Subscriber's, on *Dogue-Run* in *Fairfax*, on Sunday the 9th Instant, the following Negroes, *viz.*

Peros, 35 or 40 Years of Age, a well-set Fellow, of about 5 Feet 8 Inches high, yellowish Complexion, with a very full round Face, and full black Beard, his Speech is something slow and broken, but not in so great a Degree as to render him remarkable · He had on when he went away, a dark colour'd Cloth Coat, a white Linen Waistcoat, white Breeches and white Stockings.

Jack, 30 Years (or thereabouts) old, a slim, black, well made Fellow, of near 6 Feet high, a small Face, with Cuts down each Cheek, being his Country Marks, his Feet are large (or long) for he requires a great Shoe : The Cloathing he went off in cannot be well ascertained, but it is thought in his common working Dress, such as Cotton Waistcoat (of which he had a new One) and Breeches, and Osnabrig Shirt.

Neptune, aged 25 or 30, well-set, and of about 5 Feet 8 or 9 Inches high, thin jaw'd, his Teeth stragling and fil'd sharp, his Back, if rightly remember'd, has many small Marks or Dots running from both Shoulders down to his Waistband, and his Head was close shaved : Had on a Cotton Waistcoat, black or dark colour'd Breeches, and an Osnabrig Shirt.

Cupid, 23 or 25 Years old, a black well made Fellow, 5 Feet 8 or 9 Inches high, round and full faced, with broad Teeth before, the Skin of his Face is coarse, and inclined to be pimply, he has no other distinguishable Mark that can be recollected ; he carried with him his common working Cloaths, and an old Osnabrigs Coat made Frockwise.

The two last of these Negroes were bought from an *African* Ship in *August* 1759, and talk very broken and unintelligible *English* ; the second one, *Jack*, is Countryman to those, and speaks pretty good *English*, having been several Years in the Country. The other, *Peros*, speaks much better than either, indeed has little of his Country Dialect left, and is esteemed a sensible judicious Negro.

As they went off without the least Suspicion, Provocation, or Difference with any Body, or the least angry Word or Abuse from their Overseers, 'tis supposed they will hardly lurk about in the Neighbourhood, but steer some direct Course (which cannot even be guessed at) in Hopes of an Escape : Or, perhaps, as the Negro *Peros* has lived many Years about *Williamsburg*, and *King-William* County, and *Jack* in *Middlesex*, they may possibly bend their Course to one of those Places.

Whoever apprehends the said Negroes, so that the Subscriber may readily get them, shall have, if taken up in this County, Forty Shillings Reward, beside what the Law allows ; and if at any greater Distance, or out of the Colony, a proportionable Recompence paid them, by

George Washington.

N. B. If they should be taken separately, the Reward will be proportioned.

—August 20, 1761, *Maryland Gazette*

Coat, a white Linen Waistcoat, white Breeches and white Stockings' that Peros wore. Sunday being a day off for slaves, the four escapers would not have been missed until nightfall or the next day; and the sight of four men walking down a road in good clothing would not have aroused much suspicion because many masters allowed slaves to leave the plantation on Sundays to visit relatives or trade in Alexandria." Careful planning aside, the slaves did not make it to safety. According to Wiencek, they were discovered and sent back to Mount Vernon, though who found them and how they returned is not documented. Washington himself made just one abbreviated reference to the event in his financial records: "Prison Fees in Maryld Neptune."

Though Thomas Jefferson expressed his ambivalence over the slave trade, he, too, used the classifieds to locate his slave, Sandy, a left-handed shoemaker who, according to America's third president, had a drinking problem. "He knew slavery was evil, he called it evil and spoke out against it in a series of public forums," writes Willard Sterne Randall

---

RUN away from the subscriber in *Albemarle*, a Mulatto slave called *Sandy*, about 35 years of age, his stature is rather low, inclining to corpulence, and his complexion light; he is a shoemaker by trade, in which he uses his left hand principally; can do some coarse carpenters work, and is something of a horse jockey; he is greatly addicted to drink, and when drunk is insolent and disorderly; in his conversation, he swears much, and his behaviour is artful and knavish. He took with him a white horse, much scarred with traces, of which it is expected he will endeavour to dispose; he also carried his shoemakers tools, and will probably endeavour to get employment that way. Whoever conveys the said slave to me, in *Albemarle*, shall have 40 s. reward, if taken up within the county, 4 l. if elsewhere within the colony, and 10 l. if in any other colony, from

THOMAS JEFFERSON.

—September 21, 1769, *Virginia Gazette*

---

the runaway slave notice

Stop the Runaway.
FIFTY DOLLARS REWARD.

ELOPED from the subscriber, living near Nashville, on the 25th of June last, a Mulatto Man Slave, about thirty years old, six feet and an inch high, stout made and active, talks sensible, stoops in his walk, and has a remarkable large foot, broad across the root of the toes--will pass for a free man, as I am informed he has obtained by some means, certificates as such — took with him a drab great-coat, dark mixed body coat, a ruffled shirt, cotton home-spun shirts and overalls. He will make for Detroit, through the states of Kentucky and Ohio, or the upper part of Louisiana. The above reward will be given any person that will take him, and deliver him to me, or secure him in jail, so that I can get him. If taken out of the state, the above reward, and all reasonable expences paid--and ten dollars extra, for every hundred lashes any person will give him, to the amount of three hundred.

ANDREW JACKSON,
Near Nashville, State
of Tennessee.

—September 26, 1804, *Tennessee Gazette*

in *Thomas Jefferson: A Life*, "but he would only push so far—and then he would fall back on a way of life utterly dependent on slave labor."

Sandy's escape attempt was also not successful. He was caught, brought back to Monticello, and sold several years later.

Andrew Jackson also depended heavily on slave labor. According to Robert Remini, in his book *Andrew Jackson and the Course of American Empire, 1767–1821,* his inventory of human property progressively increased over the years: "The 1820 census reported that he held 44 slaves, of whom 27 were male and 17 female. By the time Jackson became President of the United States there were 95 slaves at the Hermitage. A few years later that number totaled 150." In late September of 1804, and then again in October and November, Jackson searched for one of his slaves in the pages of the *Tennessee Gazette.* He didn't offer up a name, but he could describe the shape of his slave's feet from memory. The bonus reward at the end of his notice gives us a sense of Jackson's position on corporal punishment.

In a reversal of roles, one United States president found himself the subject of a runaway notice. Forty-one years before Andrew Johnson would hold America's top executive office—abruptly promoted to that position from his vice-presidential station after Abraham Lincoln was shot and killed—Johnson appeared in a fugitive apprentice advertisement. Johnson grew up in a poor family; when he was nine years old, he was apprenticed to a tailor in Raleigh, North Carolina. In exchange for food, clothing, board, and training, apprentices were legally bound to serve their masters until the age of twenty-one, but it was often grueling work with unjust conditions, and countless apprentices, like slaves as well as indentured servants, took flight. James Selby, the tailor Andrew Johnson and his older brother worked for, inserted the following notice in a local Raleigh newspaper.

the runaway slave notice

Ten Dollars Reward.

RAN AWAY from the Subscriber, on the night of the 15th instant, two apprentice boys, legally bound, named WILLIAM and ANDREW JOHNSON. The former is of a dark complexion, black hair, eyes, and habits. They are much of a height, about 5 feet 4 or 5 inches. The latter is very fleshy freckled face, light hair, and fair complexion. They went off with two other apprentices, advertised by Messrs. Wm. & Chas. Fowler. When they went away, they were well clad—blue cloth coats, light colored homespun coats, and new hats, the maker's name in the crown of the hats, is Theodore Clark. I will pay the above Reward to any person who will deliver said apprentices to me in Raleigh, or I will give the above Reward for Andrew Johnson alone.

All persons are cautioned against harboring or employing said apprentices, on pain of being prosecuted.

JAMES J. SELBY, Tailor
Raleigh, N.C. June 24, 1824

—June 25, 1824, *Star, and North Carolina Gazette*

The ad did not retrieve the brothers, though Andrew Johnson eventually returned to Raleigh on his own. He searched out his former boss and tried to fulfill his apprenticeship, but James Selby would not take him back. Unable to find work locally, Andrew moved to Greeneville, Tennessee, opened his own tailor shop, got involved in politics, and began his slow ascent to the White House.

A Curious Moment in Classified History

Crispus Attucks is considered the first casualty of the American Revolution. Two decades before the Boston Massacre, the scene of his death, William Brown of Framingham, Massachusetts, posted this ad in search of him.

RAN-away from his Master *William Brown* of *Framingham*, on the 30th of *Sept.* last, a Molatto Fellow, about 27 Years of Age, named *Crispas*, 6 Feet two Inches high, short curl'd Hair, his Knees nearer together than common; had on a light colour'd Bearskin Coat, plain brown Fustian Jacket, or brown all-Wool one, new Buckskin Breeches, blue Yarn Stockings, and a check'd woollen Shirt.

Whoever shall take up said Run-away, and convey him to his abovesaid Master, shall have *ten Pounds*, old Tenor Reward, and all necessary Charges paid. And all Masters of Vessels and others, are hereby caution'd against concealing or carrying off said Servant on Penalty of the Law. *Boston*, *October* 2. 1750.

—October 2, 1750, *Boston Gazette, or Weekly Journal*

EMANCIPATION

As each northern state voted to outlaw slavery, the printing of runaway notices tapered off. This didn't happen abruptly, but followed the sluggish and painstaking process of emancipation carried out by each state independently. In the two northern states with the largest slave populations—New York and New Jersey—a true end to slavery took decades. New York passed "an act for the gradual abolition of slavery" in 1799; New Jersey waited until 1804. The repercussions were astounding. A son born in New York after July 4, 1799, was forced to serve his mother's master until the age of twenty-eight; a daughter, until the age of twenty-five. Slaves born before that date would have to wait until July 4, 1827, when New York legislation finally abolished slavery in earnest. New Jersey's time table was more frustrating. According to Graham Russell Hodges and Alan Edward Brown, co-authors of *Pretends to Be Free,* "Fugitive slave notices appeared in Monmouth County, New Jersey as late as 1840 when Daniel Conover of Middletown, advertised the flight of two slave brothers, Aaron and Abram, an indication of how flight remained a popular method for seizing freedom for northern blacks long after the American Revolution."

It took much longer in the South. Even though Congress officially banned slavery on January 31, 1865, with the passing of the Thirteenth Amendment, at least some southern planters didn't officially free their slaves until spring, after Lee surrendered to Grant on April 9 of that year. Although the runaway-slave notice lost its immediate purpose, the format did not entirely disappear. In the South, black codes drafted after the Civil War replaced slave codes. Further penalizing the poor, vagrancy laws fined blacks without jobs or permanent homes; those unable to come up with the money were committed involuntarily to bound labor. Unclaimed orphans were hired out to whites (oftentimes, former owners), and forced to work under the control of their masters until a designated age of maturity. A full decade after the close of the Civil War, Starkey Redditt offered a penny reward for his teenage apprentice, Mack.

PERSONAL—I will pay a reward of one cent, and no thanks to the man who earns it, for the apprehension and return to me, at my residence, 3 miles east of Bartlett, of a colored boy (mulatto) about 17 years of age, known as Mack Redditt, he having been apprenticed to me, and has absconded from my custody and control. And I hereby warn all persons from harboring said runaway apprentice.
my1 1w   **STARKEY REDDITT.**

—May 6, 1875, *Daily Memphis Avalanche*

Following the Civil War, newly freed slaves long since separated from their loved ones took advantage of the same advertising tool once used against them, and sought each other in the pages of African-American newspapers. Sold to different owners in various states over the years, some hadn't seen or heard from each other in decades.

The renaming practice emerged once again, as many free African Americans celebrated and confirmed their freedom by choosing last names for the first time. "Indeed for many freed-people the naming or renaming process was as much about reclaiming what they and their forebears had made in slavery as creating something new in freedom," writes Ira Berlin, in *Generations of Captivity.* "Following an ancient tradition, some identified themselves with trades or skills, taking surnames—or 'titles,'

$200 REWARD—The subscriber will pay the above reward to any one who will bring to him, or to this office, his grandchild, of about five year of age. His father's name was Jacob McKenzie, and his mother's name was Salina, (by the child called Nena.) The mother was formerly held by Jacob Barrett, of Linton, Ga, and hired by Dr. Carr, of Washington co., Ga. Soon after General Sherman's army entered Savannah, the mother and child started for the same place. At Winsboro the mother was taken sick, and placed the child in charge of a gentleman who had but one leg, and who promised to take the child to Savannah for her. The gentleman's name is unknown; but if the facts stated shall be sufficient to identify the child, the kindness of the one who restores him will ever be remembered in addition to the above reward being paid.

ISAAC WILLIAMS
50 Wolf St., Charleston, SC

—December 16, 1865, *South Carolina Leader*

as black people called them—like Barber, Cooper, Carpenter, Smith, or Taylor. Others ennobled themselves with the name King or Prince. While still others called themselves Black or Brown—markers of the obvious—others took the name White, perhaps presuming that the privileges of color would follow the name." A changed name—a signal of freedom—must have inadvertently complicated the search for lost loved ones. To help spread the word, those placing ads frequently asked ministers to read their notices aloud in America's houses of worship.

INFORMATION WANTED BY A MOTHER CONCERNING HER CHILDREN.

Mrs. Elizabeth Williams, who now resides in Marysville, California, was formally owned, together with her children, viz: Lydia, William, Allen, and Parker, by one John Petty, who lived about six miles from the town of Woodbury, Franklin County, Tennessee. At that time she was the wife of Sandy Rucker, and was familiarly known as Betsy—sometimes called Betsy Petty.

About twenty-five years ago, the mother was sold to Mr. Marshal Stroud, by whom, some twelve or fourteen years later, she was, for the second time, purchased by him, and taken to Arkansas. She has never seen the above named children since. Any information given concerning them, however, will be very gratefully received by one whose love for her children survives the bitterness and hardships of many long years spent in slavery.

Preachers in the neighborhood of Woodbury, Tennessee, are especially requested to make inquiry, and communicate any information they may deem valuable, either by letter, or through the columns of the "Recorder."

—March 17, 1866, *Christian Recorder* (Philadelphia)

Information Wanted.

INFORMATION is wanted of my mother, whom I left in Fauquier county, Va., in 1844, and I was sold in Richmond, Va., to Saml. Copeland. I formerly belonged to Robert Rogers. I am very anxious to hear from my mother, and any information in relation to her whereabouts will be thankfully received. My mother's name was Betty, and was sold by Col. Briggs to James French.—Any information by letter, addressed to the Colored Tennessean, Box 1150, will be thankfully received.

THORNTON COPELAND

—October 14, 1865, *Colored Tennessean*

INFORMATION WANTED

Of my son Charles Blackwell. He was sold from me in Lancaster county, Virginia, ten years ago, when quite young. He was sold from the estate of Mr. Joseph Beacham to Mr. Lewis Dix, and then taken to Mississippi. I am an old man and need the companionship of my son. Any assistance in securing information will be thankfully received. Ministers in Missisippi and throughout the entire country will please read in their churches. Address information to my address,

LEWIS BLACKWELL.

Lancaster Court House, Virginia.

—May 22, 1869, *Christian Recorder* (Philadelphia)

Nuts	Pilgrim
Saw and Mallet	Water But
Turnips	Fox

CHAPTER 3

Information Wanted

OF ROSA QUIROLLA, an Italian girl, about 10 years old. She left Cincinnati in November last, in company with an organ grinder named AGOSTINO PASTINE, a tall, swarthy man of about 22 years of age. The girl has the peculiarity of playing the Tambourine with her left hand. The parties were reported to be in the State of Missouri in February last. The girl's parents are fearful that wrong and guilt may have happened to her; and a liberal reward will be paid for any information about her, addressed to STEPHEN PODESTA, 12 Green st, Boston, Ms.   j16

—July 16, 1853, *Boston Pilot*

When an extended period or moment in history made it challenging, or just impossible, for loved ones to stay together, clusters of "Information Wanted" notices appeared in print.

The slave trade generated a specific need for this kind of advertising; so did voluntary immigration, which separated family members and friends over long stretches of time. Before the invention of the telephone—Alexander Graham Bell patented the technology in 1876, but it would take time before the average household installed the convenience—keeping in touch meant social visits or letter writing. If a party moved and failed to forward a new address, the lapse in communication could last years. The notice columns helped bridge some of those gaps, providing a public bulletin board for immigrants, a central place to announce arrivals, or to search out those lost somewhere along the way.

And this method of mass communication bridged more than gaps of silence: a diverse cross-section of society used the want ads to search out crucial pieces of information. When children strayed away or were kidnapped, parents relied on the classifieds to help bring their young ones back. A gale in the forecast, the capsizing of a boat, and the drowning of a fisherman could have all led to a newspaper notice a day or two later, posted by a "disconsolate" wife after her husband failed to return home that stormy night. When private property was stolen or vandalized, owners sought bystander information in the classifieds. For years, the "information wanted" notice functioned as a searchlight for witnesses, a broadcast medium capable of reaching across great social, economic, and geographic distances.

THE IRISH IN AMERICA

> **O**F MARY SUMMETS, nine years old, who
> sailed from Liverpool the 4th of May last, in
> the ship "Arctic," for New York. She came in com-
> pany with, and under the protection of Maryanne
> Treanor, daughter of Patrick Treanor, of Clifden.
> Miss Treanor had a brother living with Mr. Bishop
> of Louisville, Ky. Should this notice come to her,
> she will please inform me immediately by letter
> what became of Mary Summers on landing in New
> York, or did she ever arrive there? Also, any other
> person giving information of the child, will much
> relieve the great grief and anxiety of her discon-
> solate, widowed mother. Address Rev. R. P.
> O'NEILL, Parkersburgh, Va.
>
> —December 17, 1853, *Boston Pilot*

In 1845, Ireland's potato crop showed the first signs of decay.
Over the next few years, the "Great Famine," the worst potato
blight in Irish history, prompted a massive surge of transatlantic
movement. Between 1845 and 1855, roughly one and a half million
Irish men, women, and children packed their bags and left for the
shores of the United States. This exodus can be loosely characterized by one collective goal, described by Kerby Miller in *Emigrants
and Exiles:* "In the pre-Famine decades emigrants sought 'independence,' economic improvement, in a land fabled for opportunity
and abundance. During the Famine, however, most emigrants as-
pired merely to survive."

The ocean crossing was long and dangerous. Disease swept
through the ships and claimed the lives of the weaker ones. Ventilation

information wanted

was poor, there were few toilets to speak of, and some vessels neglected to provide any food at all. Despite such dangerously crude conditions, many fled for their lives and boarded sailing ships bound for America. But families did not always make that journey together. In fact, the majority of Irish emigrants in the mid-nineteenth century travelled to the United States on their own, leaving their families behind. "Single persons were more mobile, more able to move about searching for work," writes Ruth-Ann Harris in *The Search for Missing Friends.* "Thus the Irish were ideally suited to nineteenth-century America's rapidly growing economy, which required a low-skilled, expendable labor force." With the migration of family members often staggered, and those making the move overwhelmingly poor, staying connected to relatives was difficult, but essential.

Ads like Andrew Sleavin's, opposite, appeared in mainstream American dailies, but they found a target audience in publications

---

Information Wanted Of MARY MUNSTER, native of Town Rath, near Drogheda, co. Louth, who came to America May, 1845—when last heard from, (by letter last spring), she was living within 75 miles of Boston, but did not mention the name of the place, and supposed to be in Boston at present. Any information respecting her will be thankfully received by her brother, Patrick Munster, Watertown, Ms.

—October 28, 1848, *Boston Pilot*

Information Wanted Of PATRICK FITZGERALD, a native of Ownscoil, co. Kerry, who came to America about three years ago, leaving his wife and one child in Ireland. He was seen in Boston 3 weeks ago. Any information respecting his whereabouts at present will be thankfully received by his wife, Bridget, who has lately arrived in Boston, in search of him. Direct to her, care of Mr. David Kelly, 59 Eliot street, Boston, Ms.

—July 14, 1849, *Boston Pilot*

> NOTICE—ELLEN SLEAVEN, aged about 19 years, left DONEGAL County, IRELAND, in the summer of 1847, for America. She stopped for a few months in Coburg, C.W., and went thence to New-York city in search of her brother. Since when her friends have received no tidings from her. Any information respecting her present whereabouts will be gratefully received by an afflicted brother. ADDRESS ANDREW SLEAVIN, Copenhagen, Lewis Co., New-York.
>
> —December 20, 1851,
> *New-York Daily Times*

catering specifically to the Irish-American community. Beginning in 1831 and continuing for the next eighty-five years, the *Boston Pilot* ran "Information Wanted" ads under the simple heading "Missing Friends." In 1850, the *Pilot,* familiarly known as the "Irishman's Bible," claimed circulation "in every town in the United States, Canada, British Provinces, Mexico, &c., where there is an Irishman." It offered words of advice to newly arrived immigrants, posted upcoming ship schedules, and covered big and small news from Ireland (including birth, death, and marriage announcements, current events, and political developments), as well as Irish-related dispatches from America. These words, written to the editor of the *Pilot* by a loyal subscriber, spoke to the paper's benefits and influence: "That all Irishmen should be interested in the circulation of your paper, through the length and breadth of this great continent, there is not a doubt, promulgating as it does, such wholesome doctrines for their political, spiritual, and temporal welfare, and 'Shewing the emigrant where he can settle best, with his back turned to Britain, his face to the West.' "

INFORMATION WANTED Of JOHN CALNAN, native of co. Cork, who about 8 yrs ago was married by the Rev. George Hay, of St. Andrew's, Upper Canada, to Miss Anne McLellan, a young Scotchwoman from Glengarry. He left her for the States about last September twelve months. When last heard from he was in Bedford County, Virginia. She and her four young children have been left entirely dependent on her friends, who were not pleased with her for having abandoned Presbyterianism and become a Catholic. Any information respecting him will be thankfully received by her, care of Rev. Mr. McDonald, V.G., St. Raphael's, or Rev. Mr. Begley, Alexandria, U.C.* If John has any means spared, she expects that he will without delay send some money to the care of the above named Rev. gentlemen for his wife and little children.

—March 22, 1851, *Boston Pilot*

OF JAMES FOLEY, and his wife, ELLEN O'BRIEN, formerly of Thorny Bridge, co. Tipperary. Their three children, John, Michael and Mary, and their aunt, Mary O'Brien, are in New Orleans some time. The children are anxious to hear from their parents. They are supposed to reside near Brandon, Ms. Any one knowing them will confer a favor by showing them this, that they may send money to the children, who have all been sick and wish to get away out of this place. Address care of THOMAS O'DONNELL, Bookseller, New Orleans, for JOHN FOLEY.

—May 24, 1851, *Boston Pilot*

BOY LOST! OF PATK MAHER, a boy aged 9 years, who in company with his brothers arrived in Detroit, Mich about April 15th, from Boston, on their way to their father, Thomas Maher, in Chicago, Ill. His brothers missed him at Detroit—Information will be received by JV Clarke, Esq Chicago, Ill; John Madden, 588 Commercial street, Boston; or Enoch Train & Co, Boston, Mass.

—June 3, 1854, *Boston Pilot*

---

* Sometimes the contact person noted was someone other than the advertiser. Relatives and friends served as point persons, but so did booksellers, postmasters, lawyers, clergymen, and other recognizable members of the local community. The gentlemen Anne McLellan listed in her advertisement were likely prominent figures in their respective communities and easy to locate.

Usually readers could find the most current notices for "Missing Friends" on the back page of the paper. At the peak of Irish immigration, hundreds of these ads were packed into a single issue, often spilling into several columns' worth of print space. For years, it cost an advertiser $1.00 to place such a notice (which appeared three times); the price went up to $1.50 in August of 1864. By sending off that price in gold, readers living in "England, Ireland, or Scotland, or any part of the world" could also make use of the service. "There is very little risk in sending gold in a letter," the newspaper reassured its long-distance clients, "if stitched into it, or placed between a small piece of pasteboard or card."

A significant Irish population settled in the Boston area, but New York City became home to the nation's largest Irish-American community. According to the U.S. Census Bureau, roughly 130,000 Irish immigrants lived in New York City in 1850; ten years later that number had grown to 200,000. With a total city population of approximately 800,000 in 1860, one out of every four New Yorkers came from Ireland. After its launch in 1849, the *Irish-American* ministered to that growing community.

INFORMATION WANTED
Of MICHAEL FINAN, a native of Sligo, Ireland, who left his wife in Louisville, Ky, on the 17th of December, 1854, for the purpose of getting work, intending to be absent only a short time, since when he was not been heard of. He had the initials of his name in blue letters on his left arm. Any intelligence of him, whether living or dead, will be thankfully received by his wife Bridget Finan, at 485 Washington street, New York.

Cincinnati, St. Louis, and New Orleans papers, will confer a favor on his afflicted wife by copying the above.

—February 16, 1856, *Irish-American*

Like Michael Finan, many men left their families "for the purpose of getting work," pursuing jobs wherever they could find them. In the words of the famous journalist Thomas D'Arcy McGee, Irishmen provided "the hands which led Lake Erie downwards to the sea, and wedded the strong Chesapeake to the Gentle Delaware, and carried the roads of the East out to the farthest outpost of the West." In the newspaper layout, help-wanted notices recruiting day laborers for long-term construction projects in far-flung locations, the cause of many separations, ran strikingly close to advertisements for "Missing Friends."

INFORMATION WANTED
Of JOHN CROWLEY, about 50 years of age, who left Baltimore last August with the intention of going to work on some of the Railroads in Pennsylvania, and not since heard from. Information respecting him will be thankfully received by his wife, CATHERINE CROWLEY, Canton, near Baltimore, Md.
—March 26, 1853, *Boston Pilot*

Construction work like the kind John Crowley set off to find was dangerous, and a death on the job could have explained a gap of silence between a husband and wife. Other immigrants simply didn't want to look back after leaving their families behind. For the one deserted, the reason for the prolonged absence was not always clear.

INFORMATION WANTED
of JOHN DOLAN, formerly of the parish of Taughmaconnell, co. Roscommon, who emigrated to America in the spring of 1840, leaving behind him a wife and three helpless children, without any means whatever for support. He has never sent them any assistance, and at length the poor wife with her children has arrived in search of him. It is supposed he is in St. John, N.B., or in the British Provinces. Any information respecting him will be thankfully received by his poor wife, Margaret Dolan (otherwise Finneron), addressed to Mr. John Carberry, Mill Dam, Roxbury, Ms.
—August 30, 1845, *Boston Pilot*

Parents left children, but children also did the leaving. They left home to chase work, follow or find a parent, enlist in the army, work at sea, or perhaps to escape a cheerless family life.

INFORMATION WANTED OF THOMAS LEONARD, a boy of twelve years old, who left his fathers house on the 11th inst, about half past five on the afternoon of said day, with the intention of going for a pail of water, and has not been seen by his parents since, all the information we have of him was that he was seen next morning in Tremont, opposite Broomfield st. The boy has deserted his home through fear of his father, who said he would whip him when he returned with the water. He wore a silver gray jacket, broke on both elbows, and pantaloons and vest similar to the jacket, a comforter on his neck, and a cloth cap, light hair, pale in the face, a long nose and countenance. Any person who has harbored the boy will be kind enough to send word to his father, PATRICK LEONARD, and direct to MICHAEL CUM-MISKEY, boot and shoe store, Merrimack st. opposite Trull's distillery will be suitably rewarded and many thanks from his parents.
PATRICK LEONARD.

—March 7, 1846, *Boston Pilot*

INFORMATION WANTED, Dublin. OF Thomas Carr, a native of Dublin, Ireland, who left home on the 13th of January last, without the consent or knowledge of his parents. He wrote from Liverpool saying, by the time his letter was received, he would be crossing the Atlantic. He is about 5 feet 4 inches in height, slight and delicate in appearance, very light brown hair, long nose, grey eyes, a respectable and well-looking boy, and about 14 years of age. When he left home he wore a blue pilo coat drab cloth trousers, and a black jerry hat. Should any person, seeing this, convey intelligence of his whereabouts to James Nolan, 638 Greenwich street, New York, it will be esteemed as a great favor, or should the boy himself call there, he will hear of something to his advantage.

—April 4, 1868, *Irish-American*

The "Information Wanted" advertisement served an important function for Irish-American immigrants: according to Patrick Donahoe, the editor of the *Boston Pilot,* "three-fourths of those advertised for are found." Although that is a hard statistic to verify, we know that some searches did meet satisfying results. In March of 1854, for example, John Hannigan looked for his cousins in the *Pilot.*

OF JOHN, MATHEW & MICHAEL TIERNEY, and their sisters, MARGARET & JOHANA, natives of Ballinahinch, parish of Knocklong, co Limerick; supposed to be somewhere in New York, or its vicinity Information of them will be received by their cousin, JOHN HANNIGAN, Hermann, Gasconade co, Missouri.   m4

—March 4, 1854, *Boston Pilot*

The following month, he sent this note of encouragement to the paper, one of many such success stories reprinted in its pages: "I have received satisfactory information of friends who I have not seen nor heard of for nearly twenty years. A good proof that any such information cannot be obtained through any other channel so expeditious as by advertising in the *Pilot.*"

Eyewitness News

In the nineteenth century, generations before the evening news, the newspaper was indeed the most expeditious channel of broadcast, the quickest way to reach the greatest number of people. The advertising insert, small as it was, functioned as a crime-solving tool, used by citizens, police departments, and private investigators alike to engage the public in a search for clues. After Abraham Lincoln was shot in the Ford Theatre on April 14, 1865, the government offered $100,000 for the collective arrests of John Wilkes Booth and two of his accomplices. This private advertiser promised his own additional incentive:

REWARDS.

A REWARD OF $75 WILL BE PAID, IN ADDITION to the sum already offered, for the arrest of the villain J. Wilkes Booth, who assassinated Abraham Lincoln, late President of the United States, at Ford's theatre, Washington, D. C., on the evening of the 14th of April, 1865.
GEORGE WM. MATTHEWS,
Williamsburg, L. I., N. Y.

—April 19, 1865, *New York Herald*

Famous cases like Lincoln's left behind tracks in the classifieds, but more often, the plight of the common advertiser showed up there. When robbers and vandals snatched belongings, victims sought justice and closure in the classifieds. If, by chance, the thief's identity was known, "publick exposure" could be threatened by the poster, a move guaranteed to stain a reputation so valued in a tight-knit community. Like lost and found advertisements, these classifieds tell us what was considered valuable to the owners, but they also make known what thieves deemed worthy enough to steal in the first place.

information wanted

TAKEN from Mrs. *Thayer's* boarding-house on Thursday evening, the 9th instant, a new GREEN SILK UMBRELLA, with a wide coloured edge; the owner's name was cut on the handle and written on the Silk. The person who took it is well known, and unless it is returned immediately (in any way he may choose) his name shall be publickly exposed.

June 17.

—June 17, 1814, *Rhode-Island American, and General Advertiser*

$3 Reward.

Whereas on the night of Friday last or early on Saturday morning, some evil disposed and wickedly inclined person or persons, did feloniously steal, take away, and carry off, ONE HIVE OF BEES from the garden of DANIEL TOWER. The above reward will be given to any person who will give such information so that the offender or offenders maybe brought to justice and punished according to law.

Sept. 21 1835   48—3

—October 6, 1835, *Tuscarawas Advocate* (Ohio)

---

5 Dollars Reward.

I WILL pay the above reward for such evidence as will convict the thief who stole a Buffalo Skin from my sleigh on the evening of the 26th of December, while under the Shed near the Grist-mill in Exeter. It was marked by a small portion of the hair being rubbed off near the fore shoulder. JOSEPH H. MELCHER.

Hampton Falls, Jan. 5, 1836.

—January 12, 1836, *Exeter News-Letter and Rockingham County Advertiser* (New Hampshire)

$25 REWARD will be paid for the detection of the cowardly thief, who is in the habit of sneaking and creeping up to the door of No. 10, City Hall Place, and stealing the Sun newspaper from under the door. The above reward will be paid for the information left at the Sun office: and a regular roasting is promised the low, guilty, niggardly thief.   28f3*

—February 29, 1840, *New York Sun*

TEN DOLLARS REWARD.—My little son, while out shooting in the neighborhood of Hollywood Cemetery, was accosted by three Irishmen, one of whom asked him to let him shoot, and at the same time picked the gun from his hand and made off. I will give the above reward for the conviction of the thief, or $2 50 for the return of the gun, which was a small, newly stocked, single-barrelled one, with the name of S. Sutherland stamped on the lock.   R. B. TYLER,

mh 9—3t*   North side Basin.

—March 9, 1852, *Daily Dispatch* (Richmond, Virginia)

$10 Reward.

FOR any information that will lead to the detection of the persons who took a quantity of cranberries from the Swamp belonging to the subscriber near the north head of the Long Pond, within a few days.

a27   GEORGE EASTON.

—October 12, 1858, *Nantucket Enquirer* (Massachusetts)

Information Wanted.

CONCERNING a One-Horse WOOD WAGON taken from my residence, by one of Gen. Wheeler's command, on the 11th inst., for the purpose of conveying a corpse to Augusta. A liberal reward will be paid for its restoration, or information which will lead to it.

                                    W. W. FINLEY.

feb 25   3t*   Aiken, S. C.

—February 26, 1865, *Daily Constitutionalist* (Augusta, Georgia)

A subset of crime-fighting advertising was devoted solely to the search for eyewitnesses. These advertisers cast their nets wide, hoping that the right person, one who was "there," might be tracked down and interviewed. In the hunt for a bystander, a scene from history unfolds before us; years later, we become the new line of witnesses, not to the actual events, but to the fact that these incidents ever happened at all.

NOTICE—SHOULD THIS MEET THE EYE OF ANY person who was on the ferry boat on Friday night, January 27, coming from Brooklyn, at half-past twelve o'-clock, on the Fulton ferry, Brooklyn side, when the cry of man overboard was made, by calling at Coulter, Krapp & Co's, No 10 Front street, and tell what they know, will receive the thanks of a distressed family.

—February 7, 1865,
New York Herald

$25 REWARD—WANTED, AS A WITNESS, the man who, on Wednesday morning, Sept. 19th, 1866 between 7½ and 8 o'clock, had a dispute with Gottleib Williams, a lame man, on the corner of Twelfth and Noble or Willow streets. The above reward will be paid by the undersigned to any one (other than the man himself) who will give notice of the whereabouts of the said person. No personal liability need be apprehended, as his testimony only is required. THOMAST J. WORRELL, Attorney-at-Law, 433 Walnut street, Phila.

—October 8, 1866,
Public Ledger (Philadelphia)

That parents also used this method of communication when their children were stolen or went astray is a powerful testament to the role these small ads played in times of crisis. Slave owners had long turned to the newspaper notice to track down runaways. And immigrant communities understood and depended on the format's power to connect, using those columns like we use the phone book or even online search engines today. But reliance on

CHILD LOST—A negro boy named PETER, about four years and six months old, strayed off from his mother on Tuesday last, and has not since been heard from. When he left, he had on no pants, but a short sack. He has a scar about the size of a quarter dollar over the right eye. Any information respecting him will be gratefully received by his mother, at Mr. James Moore's, on 14th street, near Mayo's Bridge.

—May 6, 1852, *Daily Dispatch* (Richmond, Virginia)

MISSING SINCE THE 17TH ULTIMO—A BOY ABOUT six years of age, fair hair, blue eyes, dressed in gray summer pants, and plaid loose jacket; when last seen was playing on pier 4, North river; any information leading to his recovery, will confer a lasting favor to his distressed parents. A suitable reward and all expenses incurred, will be paid by CORNELIUS McGRATH, 23 West street.

—March 4, 1855, *New York Herald*

MYSTERIOUS DISAPPEARANCE.—LEFT his lodgings a short time since, a young man of rather prepossessing appearance, dark eyes and florid complexion, hair dark brown and inclined to curl. When last seen he was dressed in a broadcloth coat, peppered breeches, and silk hat. Any information concerning him, left either at the Granite hotel, Lester place, or at this office, will be thankfully received.

P.S. *A very curious kind of written poem* has been found in his room in his own handwriting. I should be obliged if some of our best critics would call and examine this queer poem.

PROPRIETOR OF GRANITE HOTEL

—October 18, 1860, *New York World*

INFORMATION WANTED— Of my niece, who left my house on Wednesday, the 10th of February. She had on when she left a dark dress, trimmed with green ; red plaid shawl, and a calico slat bonnet. She has very black hair and eyes. The above-named was disappointed a short time since in marriage, and the impression prevails that she has drowned herself. Any information in regard to her will be thankfully received by her aunt, at the corner of Smith and Clay streets.

EVL

—February 15, 1864, *Daily Dispatch* (Richmond, Virginia)

these advertisements extended far beyond the confines of any one specific community or set of circumstances.

Today, there are more efficient systems of mass communication in place: television, radio, the Internet, emergency highway alert systems, etc. In a much larger world, with a growing number of media sources to navigate, the search for a missing person now begs for more than an inch or two of buried newsprint.

But though it may no longer function as a first line of defense when a family member disappears, the "Information Wanted" posting still holds crime-solving capabilities. Hit-and-run accidents, for example, continue to compel advertisers to seek first-hand

---

LEFT the house of the subscriber, on the 8th instant, a Boy of colour, by the name of WILLIAM KINNICUTT, alias WILLIAM WEEKES, aged about 14 years old. He wore away a short jacket and trowsers of home-made cotton.—It is expected he has wandered away and cannot find his way back, or that some ill-minded person has persuaded him to leave his home. Whoever will give information where he is, will confer a particular favour on his afflicted friends.

JOSHUA WEEKES

—Friday, May 12, 1809, *American* (Rhode Island)

INFORMATION WANTED of Fran's Parks, aged between 10 and 11 years, who strayed from home on Sunday evening, about 6 o'clock. He had on striped cotton pantaloons with a patch on the seat, black cloth vest, with velvet collar, neither shoes nor hat, has a scar or mark on his left temple, is subject to fits. Any information of him will be thankfully received by his father, John Parks, at 31 Troy st.

—August 11, 1840, *New York Sun*

$25 REWARD—FOR THE RECOVERY OF THE body of a little girl aged two years. Said child was of fair complextion; she was dressed in a brown and blue worsted coat, a blue and white cap; the child was boating with her parents, when the boat was run into a barge, and upset, when about opposite Canal street, North River. The above reward will be paid to any person who may lead to the recovery of the body of the child, by applying to RICHARD LONG, 133 Norfolk street.

—May 13, 1849, *New York Herald*

accounts through the classifieds—an old-fashioned approach, perhaps, but worthwhile if just one reliable source steps forward.

HIT AND RUN ON 21st and CASTRO on 3/17 at NOON(ish)

Reply to: anon@craigslist.org
Date: 2005-03-18, 6:46PM PST
Somebody smashed the back of my parked silver Honda Civic hatchback on Thursday 3/17 at around noon at 21st and Castro. Nobody left me a note to my exasperation. Didn't anybody witness this and if so why not leave me a note...!? I am out thousands of dollars as my insurance doesnt cover this. Help me find the culprit!

—March 18, 2005 *www.craigslist.com* (San Francisco, California)

THE KIDNAPPING OF CHARLEY ROSS

LOST—A SMALL BOY, ABOUT FOUR YEARS of age, light complexion and light curly hair. A suitable reward will be given by returning him to E. L. JOYCE, Central Police Station.   *294

—July 3, 1874, *Public Ledger* (Philadelphia)

This posting resembles other missing-children advertisements from the time: a quick physical description, a reference to time frame, a brief mention of a reward. But the standard content and phrasing don't reveal the classified's historic significance. The "small boy" advertised was Charley Ross, and his abduction was the first to receive widespread public attention in America. Kidnapping existed well before this date, but the demand for a ransom was new, as was the national, even international, fascination with the crime. Charley Ross became a household name, in America and abroad, his tragic kidnapping story a cautionary tale told and retold throughout the late-nineteenth and early-twentieth centuries.

On July 1, 1874, two men convinced four-year-old Charley and his five-year-old brother, Walter, to leave the front yard of their Germantown house and step into a Philadelphia-bound wagon. The boys were taken from their suburban neighborhood to a cigar store a few miles away, where Walter was handed twenty-five cents and sent in to purchase firecrackers for the upcoming Independence Day celebration. The kidnappers chose that moment to drive off with Charley, leaving his older brother behind. With the help of a stranger, Walter returned home that evening and recounted the details of the kidnapping to his father. The police were notified, and two days later, on the third of July, the boys' father, Christian Ross, ran that first ad for Charley in the *Philadelphia Public Ledger.* He chose not to include his son's name or his own in that initial ad: he did not want to alarm his wife, Sarah, who was out of town at the time. He placed another advertisement the following day:

> $300 REWARD WILL BE PAID TO THE person returning to No. 5 North Sixth street, a small Boy, having long, curly, flaxen hair, hazel eyes, clear, light skin and round face, dressed in a brown linen suit with short skirt, broad brimmed straw hat and laced shoes. This child was lost from Germantown on Wednesday afternoon, 1st inst., between 4 and 5 o'clock. §

—July 4, 1874, *Public Ledger* (Philadelphia)

On the day this second ad appeared in the paper, Christian Ross received word from the kidnappers, a document that is now widely considered the first ransom note in American history. It was written in a messy scrawl with deliberate misspellings, but the message was clear: "you wil hav two pay us befor you git him from us, and pay us a big cent to." The "big cent" mentioned in subsequent notes amounted to twenty thousand dollars. In all, the Ross family received twenty-three ransom notes, but for a set of complicated reasons, the father did not successfully comply with the kidnappers' financial demands. Trapped between his own sense of paternal responsibility and a moral duty to protect his community and the country from these criminals and their terrorizing act, Ross did not want to "compound the felony" by giving in to the blackmail. The police not only supported this position, they pressured Ross to uphold it. As an alternative, hefty rewards were offered to the public—in newspaper notices and handbills—for the capture of the kidnappers and the safe return of the young boy. On July 23, the mayor of Philadelphia offered a twenty-thousand-dollar reward. Pinkerton's National Detective Agency promised the same amount in pamphlets widely circulated in the summer of 1874. A three-page booklet offered "a description of the child," a "description of the kidnappers," and "questions for identification," ways to positively identify the young boy: "He can recite, 'Jesus loves me, this I know, for the Bible tells me so.' Knows 'O' and 'S' of the alphabet, but no other letters. Will state his name to be Charlie Ross, but when asked if he has any other name will say, 'Charlie Brewster Ross.' "

The negotiations between Christian Ross and the kidnappers dragged on for five months. As directed, Ross promptly responded through the "personal" column of various newspapers. "Wen you get ready to bisnes with us advertise the folering in *Ledger* personals (Ros. we be ready to negociate)," read the end of their second ransom note. "We look for yu answer in *Ledger*." Ross received those words on July 6 and on the following day, he inserted the six-word notice they demanded in the *Public Ledger*.

"ROS, WE BE READY TO NEGOTIATE."

*172

Other cryptic messages, scripted by the criminals and placed diligently by Ross, would appear in the months to come. Strangers, too, posted Charley Ross–related announcements.

PERSONAL.

A NEW YORK GENTLEMAN, OF AMPLE MEANS, in the hope of saving the life of his invalid wife, who is growing insane over the Ross abduction, will pay an amount equal to the reward—viz, $20,000, for the return to him of Charles B. Ross, in order that he may restore the child to its parents. While opposed to compromising a felony, he will act squarely in this case for the above reasons. On receipt of an answer from the right parties, proposing any reasonable plan for the exchange of child and money, money and man will be ready. Business now. Address ARTHUR PURCELL, General Post office, Philadelphia.

—July 26, 1874, *The New York Herald*

There were those who believed this message was nothing more than a ploy, that a private detective hired by the editor of the *New York Herald,* James Gordon Bennett, had posted it. Such a plan, if successful, would have reflected well on that newspaper. But who placed the notice is secondary to the fact that it appeared at all. The public became emotionally intertwined with the Charley Ross story: that a woman, fictional or real, was "growing insane over the Ross abduction" was not far-fetched.

Everyone, it seems, got involved—the Ross family, the police, the public, private investigation firms. In November, an earnest

$20,000 REWARD

Has been offered for the recovery of CHARLIE BREWSTER ROSS, and for the arrest and conviction of his abductors. He was stolen from his parents in Germantown, Pa., on July 1st, 1874, by two unknown men.

DESCRIPTION OF THE CHILD.

The accompanying portrait resembles the child, but is not a correct likeness. He is about four years old; his body and limbs are straight and well formed; he has a round, full face; small chin, with noticeable dimple; very regular and pretty dimpled hands; small, well-formed neck; full, broad forehead; bright dark-brown eyes, with considerable fullness over them; clear white skin; healthy complexion; light flaxen hair, of silky texture, easily curled in ringlets when it extends to the neck: hair darker at the roots,—slight cowlick on left side where parted: very light eyebrows. He talks plainly, but is retiring, and has a habit of putting his arm up to his eyes when approached by strangers. His skin may now be stained, and hair dyed,—or he may be dressed as a girl, with hair parted in the centre.

DESCRIPTION OF THE KIDNAPPERS.

No. 1 is about thirty-five years old; five feet nine inches high; medium build, weighing about one hundred and fifty pounds; rather full, round face, florid across the nose and cheek-bones, giving him the appearance of a hard drinker; he had sandy moustache, but was otherwise clean shaved; wore eye-glasses, and had an open-faced gold watch and gold vest-chain; also, green sleeve-buttons.

No. 2 is older, probably about forty years of age, and a little shorter and stouter than his companion: he wore chin whiskers about three inches long, of a reddish-sandy color; and had a pug-nose, or a nose in some way deformed. He wore gold bowed spectacles, and had two gold rings on one of his middle fingers, one plain and one set with red stone.

Both men wore brown straw hats, one high and one low-crowned; one wore a linen duster; and, it is thought, one had a duster of gray alpaca, or mohair.

Any person who shall discover or know of any child, which there is reason to believe may be the one abducted, will at once communicate with their Chief of Police or Sheriff, who has been furnished with means for the identification of the stolen child.

Otherwise, communications by letter or telegraph, if necessary, will be directed to either of the following officers of

PINKERTON'S NATIONAL DETECTIVE AGENCY,

Viz:
BENJ. FRANKLIN, Sup't, 45 S. Third St., Philadelphia, Pa.
R. A. PINKERTON, Sup't, 66 Exchange Place, New York.
F. WARNER, Sup't, 191 and 193 Fifth Avenue, Chicago, Ill.
GEO. H. BANGS, Gen'l Sup't.

ALLAN PINKERTON.

PHILADELPHIA, September 1st, 1874.

(POST THIS UP IN A CONSPICUOUS PLACE.)

Wm. F. Murphy's Sons, Stationers, Printers, 509 Chestnut St., Phdad.

S613.F

Pinkerton's National Detective Agency circulated this one-page reward poster on September 1, 1874. (Courtesy of the Library Company of Philadelphia.)

strange red cow

attempt *was* made to pay the kidnappers, but not by Christian Ross, who by that time was recovering from a nervous breakdown. Sarah Ross's family attempted to hand over the ransom in exchange for Charley at New York City's Fifth Avenue Hotel, but the police showed up to the scene and the plan quickly dissolved.

As this was the first high-profile ransom kidnapping in America, there was no professional protocol to follow, no previous mistakes from which to learn. Sadly, Charley's story would become that mistake: he was never discovered, dead or alive. But the suspected kidnappers *were* found. Identified as William Mosher and Joseph Douglas, both were shot dead while breaking into a home in Brooklyn, New York, on December 14. Douglas confessed to the kidnapping before taking his last breath: "It's no use lying now: Mosher and I stole Charley Ross from Germantown." Mosher's brother-in-law, William Westervelt, an ex-cop in the New York City force, was suspected of conspiring with the men, and in October of 1875, over a year after Charley's abduction, he was convicted of the crime in Pennsylvania.

In spite of these dramatic developments, true closure never came to the Ross family or to the public who had paid such close attention to every hairpin turn in the story. Christian Ross searched until he died in 1897, and then his wife pushed on with the investigation. Charley Ross survived in name alone as a criminal history case study, invoked in future ransom notes and closing arguments in the courtroom. His story would haunt America for decades. "Just after Walter Ross died in 1943," writes Paula Fass in *Kidnapped,* "a Germantown paper announced that 'Philadelphia police this week, for the thousandth time, were given a tip which may turn out to be a valuable clue in the search for Charley Ross.' "

Earth.

Air.

Fire.

Water.

CHAPTER 4

Personals

J. A. R.—SARCASM AND INDIFFERENCE HAVE driven me from you. I sail in next steamer for Europe. Shall I purchase tickets for two, or do you prefer to remain to wound some other loving heart? Answer quick, or all is lost. EMELIE.

—December 18, 1865, *New York Herald*

We have come to associate personal advertising with the search for a partner, but in America's pre-telephone days, the "personal" column also served as a practical mode of person-to-person communication, a place to conduct business, leave a note for a friend, say thanks or sorry to a stranger. Mothers and fathers, unable to provide proper care for their newborns, tried to secure better homes for them through the personals. Lovers left each other ultimatums; families fought and made up; hearts were broken, mended, then shamelessly broken again. Life's dramas unfolded there alongside the dull logistics of the day. The column was wide open to interpretation, as all things *personal,* grave or trivial, could conceivably end up there.

THE LADY WHO ENCLOSED $1, ON SATURDAY last, to Dr. Duponce, at the Broadway Post Office, for a box of his golden pills, will please write again, as she neglected to give the street where to send them.

—February 20, 1855,
New York Herald

THE LADY WHO LOST HER KING CHARLES'S SPANIEL near Union square, in Broadway, yesterday morning, tenders her most cordial thanks to the gentleman who so kindly volunteered to release him from the thief, and sympathies with the young man who was knocked down in the melee.

—March 28, 1855,
New York Herald

WILL MR. JOHN O'NEILL, JR. PLEASE MEET Lieut. Chas P. at 67 Wall street, who will furnish him with further particulars concerning the last wishes of his friend, Walter DeP., of Alabama, who was killed at the battle of Ball's Bluff.

—January 22, 1862,
New York Herald

MAY MINNIE—FAREWELL, CRUEL GIRL! If not drafted, I will go as a substitute. Your scorn is harder and more pitiless to me than any Southern bullet could possibly be.

John No 1.

—August 3, 1862, *New York
Sunday Mercury*

The English coined the personals the "agony column" for all the anguish and suffering preserved in those small blocks of text. "I read nothing except the criminal news and the agony column," admitted Sir Arthur Conan Doyle's character, Sherlock Holmes, in "The Adventure of the Noble Bachelor." Holmes regularly combed the classifieds for clues, and openly admitted to their intrigue. "What a

strange red cow

TO JOHN F.G. OF H.N.—IF YOU DO NOT INTEND to break the hearts of your parents write immediately, and give your whereabouts. Remember what you yourself have felt when we lost poor little Frederick, and consider what your mother and father must suffer at present. If there is yet a spark of love in your bosom—and we think there must not be a spark, but a flame—write immediately. The heartiest welcome of father, mother, sisters, and brothers is sure to you.

—September 8, 1862,
New York Herald

X.Z.—IF YOU MUST HAVE A REASON why I refuse you, understand, then, that I cannot marry a man who wears soiled linen, has foul teeth and breath, and uses tobasco and whisky. Faugh !
GENERRA

—November 16, 1862, *New York Sunday Mercury*

I HEREBY RETURN MY THANKS TO DR. H. A. DANIELS, of 221 Sixth avenue, near Fourteenth street, for skillfully removing without pain a large foreign substance from my ear, which had troubled me for a considerable time. I can fully testify to the doctor's ability as a surgeon. GEO. BOWERYEM.

—December 21, 1862, *New York Sunday Mercury*

MR. MARTINEZ, OF THE MAISON DOREE, desires publicly to express his profound regret at the mistake in personal identity made by him in addressing a gentleman in a Madison-av. stage, opposite Stewart's, on Tuesday morning, 8th inst.

—December 9, 1863,
New-York Times

SPECIAL NOTICE—The lady who purchased a HAT from a servant girl in the Second Market on Wednesday morning for sixteen dollars will please return it, as the girl was not authorized to sell it.

J.M. EGGLESTON
Corner of First and Canal streets.

—September 8, 1864, *Daily Dispatch*
(Richmond, Virginia)

ANDREW—YOU HAVE GIVEN ME SUFFICIENT cause, I think, to make me resolve to forget you if possible; but the sight of you on Thursday has set me crazy again. How can you be so cruel? Am I never to hear from you again?

B.C.

—March 21, 1875,
New York Herald

chorus of groans, cries, and bleatings!" he once said. "What a rag-bag of singular happenings! But surely the most valuable hunting-ground that ever was given to a student of the unusual!"

PERSONAL—If the unknown friend who addressed me an anonymous letter—mailed on the 10th instant—and stated that an interview could be had on Wednesday at the Spotswood Hotel, will allow me an interview, he will further the ends of humanity and justice. I attended the Spotswood, but failed to see the grey hat, with letter A, and arm in sling.

—January 12, 1865, *Daily Dispatch* (Richmond, Virginia)

THE LADY WHO CALLED UPON ME AT MY OFFICE on a Friday afternoon some four or five weeks ago, and left a note signed "You know who," will please make herself known, as she is not recognized.

—October 21, 1865, *New York Herald*

FOR ADOPTION—A FINE FEMALE CHILD, FOUR weeks old, whose mother died at its birth, and whose father, a Frenchman, lost everything at the Portland fire. Address box 121 Herald office.

—July 16, 1866, *New York Herald*

ROSE—IT IS USELESS—YOU ARE TOO LOVELY TO be trifled with. I am married.

BENEDICT.

—August 27, 1867, *New York Herald*

WILL THE GENTLEMAN WHO PICKED UP THE little child from the ground after being run over by a grocer's wagon in Hamilton avenue, Brooklyn, on St. Patrick's Day favor the afflicted father with his address? BENJAMIN TAYLOR, 210 Van Brunt st, Brooklyn.

—March 20, 1875, *New York Herald*

A VIEW TO MATRIMONY

> ## To the LADIES.
>
> ANY young Lady, between the Age of Eighteen and Twenty-three, of a middling Stature; brown Hair; regular Features, and with a lively brisk Eye; of good Morals, and not tinctur'd with any Thing that may fully so distinguishable a Form; possessed of 3 or 400 l. entirely at her own Disposal, and where there will be no necessity of going thro' the tiresome Task of addressing Parents or Guardians for their Consent; such an one, by leaving a Line directed for A. W. at the *British Coffee-House* in Kingstreet, appointing where an Interview may be had, will meet with a Person who flatters himself that he shall not be thought disagreeable by any Lady answering the above Description.
>
> *N. B.* Profound Secrecy will be observ'd. No trifling Answers will be regarded. *Boston, Feb.* 23. 1759.
>
> —February 26, 1759, *Boston Evening-Post*

This ad for a mate, one of the first of its kind in the colonies, was inconspicuously printed between an advertisement for a lost "small brown leather purse" and a real estate notice, the offer to buy a farm with a good barn and orchard, and a well-wooded lot of land. Advertising for a spouse wasn't considered socially acceptable and "A.W." was keenly aware of that fact, but in 1759 cultural pressure to marry was strong and bachelorhood was regarded as a social aberration. Colonial legislation both ostracized and penalized single men. One of the most curious laws, passed in 1695 in Eastham, Massachusetts, declared that "every unmarried man in the township shall kill six blackbirds or three crows while he remain single; as a penalty for not doing it, shall not be married until he obey this order."

That A.W. wondered aloud about what kind of dowry he might expect was perfectly reasonable. Women held no legal, financial, or political power, and whatever sum of money or parcel of property she could bring to the relationship would fall under her husband's jurisdiction just as soon as they wed. "A woman ceased to exist if she married, for she and her spouse became one flesh and the flesh was his," explains Philip S. Foner in *Women and the American Labor Movement.* "The husband had the right to chastise his wife physically . . . and he had exclusive rights to any property she might have owned as a single woman, to her dower, and to any wages or property that might come to her while she was his wife. In short, like slave and servant women, married women, whether rich or poor, were legal nonentities." Prior to marriage, fathers held the keys to their daughters' futures. Though women typically chose their own spouses, a father's approval or disapproval could have significantly impacted the size of her dowry. A.W.'s unwillingness to go "thro' the tiresome Talk of addressing Parents or guardians for their Consent" must have seemed odd, even controversial at the time.

In spite of the stigma attached to this method of advertising, by the mid-nineteenth century, matrimonially minded notices could be spotted in rural and urban newspapers alike. Men and women, tired of the monotony of single life and presumably unable to meet suitable partners through more conventional channels—churches, friends, family, and other tight-knit social networks—tried their luck with self-advertising. Secrecy continued to be a priority: both sexes were quick to promise that "all communications will be held as sacredly confidential" and that "the real name can be withheld."

Men sought wives who could "write a plain hand," who "understood housekeeping in all of its branches," and were generally capable of making home a happy place. Females routinely looked for financially secure husbands of good moral habits, with unblemished

HUSBAND WANTED—Wanted immediately, by a good looking young woman, 20 years of age, a partner for life. The advertiser is of an amiable disposition, and possesses $500 in ready money to furnish her house and a farm, which brings in the value of $500 per annum. The title to the property is good. Her husband must be strictly temperate, regular in his habits; good disposition; of good address; and all the et ceteras which constitute a real gentleman. His property must be double the amount of the above, and his connexions respectable. Address G.O. through the Post Office. No interview can be had unless a reference in the note is given.

—January 6, 1835, *New York Sun*

MATRIMONIAL—A colored gentleman who resides in the country, where there are but few of his own color, and who has not the pleasure of a very large circle of acquaintances, and whose business is such that it demands his time and attention, is desirous of forming an acquaintance with a lady of intelligence, and who is good in acts as well as in looks; with a view to matrimony. He is a widower, about 38 years of age, and has a daughter whose age is 15 years. Can give the best reference as to character and sobriety. This notice is predicated on truth and sincerity, and none need answer but on the like basis. He hopes that any lady who is afflicted with any hereditary disease will not answer this communication. Address O.R.W., box No. 237, Bethlehem, Northampton Co., Pa.

—December 10, 1859, *Weekly Anglo-African* (New York City)

A YOUNG LADY, SEVENTEEN YEARS OF AGE, AND possessed of a moderate fortune, is desirous of opening a correspondence with some gentleman with a view to matrimony. The gentleman must not be more than twenty-five years old, and must possess a fine intellectual countenance, be of an agreeable disposition, and above all must have a love of a mustache. The young lady is compelled to adopt this mode of opening a correspondence owing to the strict surveillance under which she is placed at home. Address Ethel, Brooklyn Post office.

—May 16, 1861, *New York Herald*

MARRIAGE—A GENTLEMAN, YOUNG, WITH A FAIR portion of cash and very "large expectations," desires to make some good and handsome girl his wife. Her happiness will be his own, and the sincere object of marital relations; money no object, but youth indispensable. Old maids, widows, and ugly women over 18 need not respond to "Ye Man," Herald Office.

—March 8, 1866, *New York Herald*

characters and undoubted social positions. In some cases, references were required.

Painfully practical advertisers—tactless by today's standards—were joined by a more playful group of singles, men and women willing to expose their personal quirks, even their fetishes. Personals placed by women determined to challenge the gender expectations of the time stand out in the crowd.

A YOUNG LADY, COUNTRY BRED, BUT EASILY tamed and civilized, would like to correspond with a city gentleman, with a view to matrimony. It is necessary for him to be wealthy, and not less than forty years of age, as she would "rather be an old man's darling than a young man's slave." The advertiser is 21, and presumes her manners and appearance will recommend her to tastes not over fastidious; also a lady of position, and will expect replies from responsible parties only; therefore, triflers, take heed. Address Matilda, station D Post office.

—December 21, 1861,
New York Herald

For the Civil War soldier, the personal advertisement offered the promise of a future or, at the very least, a distraction from the present. Away from home, deprived of basic comforts, and disconnected from female companionship, the daily life of the soldier wavered between intense physical and emotional trials and extended periods of boredom. To pass the time, men gambled, penned letters home, and played baseball, and some sought "horizontal refreshments" from local prostitutes, who followed the troops. Records show that 10 percent of Union troops suffered from venereal disease, though many more on both sides actually contracted the medical condition. Advertising in the personals was a safer way to cope with loneliness.

AN OFFICER, WHO IS SUF-FERING FROM a wound, and who has recently been released from Richmond, is desirous of forming a correspondence with some lady for the purpose of cheering his drooping spirits. Address Lieut. H.V.A., Fortress Monroe, Va.

—January 22, 1862,
New York Herald

A YOUNG OFFICER OF THE UNITED STATES Army, now in the field, aged 23, is desirous of forming a correspondence with some young lady, between the ages of 16 and 22, with a view to better acquain-tance at the expiration of the war. The advertiser is not what they call a pretty man, but a plucky one and full of fun, and expects the same of the lady; nei-ther am I wealthy, but can manage to steer clear of bad rocks. Address in confidence Lieut. Henry S. W., Brooklyn (L.I.) Post office.

—March 7, 1862,
New York Herald

TO PATRIOTIC UNMAR-RIED LADIES.—I am a sol-dier, just returned from the wars. Have lost a leg, but expect to get a cork one; have a useless arm, but will be called brave for it; was once good-looking, but am now scarred all over. If any patriotic young lady will marry me, why fall in line! The applicant must be moderately handsome, have an excellent education, play on the piano and sing; and a competency will not be objectionable. One with these requirements would, doubtless, se-cure my affections. Address Capt. F.A.B., MERCURY Office.

—November 9, 1862, *New York Sunday Mercury*

Matrimony—A good looking young man, a soldier, wishes to correspond with a young lady on the shady side of fifty, with a view to mat-rimony. None but those who are good at patching breeches and darning stockings need apply. Address for one month, A.A.C., Mess No. 6, Maga-zine street.

—March 16, 1863, *Letter H* (Camp Parapet, Louisiana)

Attention, Ladies! Two "Gay and Festive" lads, members of Co. A. 8th Regt. Maine Vols respectfully solicit the corre-spondence of a number of Loyal and Patriotic young ladies of Franklin County with a view to fun and mutual improvement. Ladies between the ages of 16 and 21 most desirable. None with "secesh"* sentiment de-sired. Address FRANK BERNARD and CHARLES KANE Co., A. 8th, Regt. Maine Vet. Vol. Richmond.

—May 24, 1865, *Farmington Chronicle* (Maine)

---

* For these Union soldiers, politics was a potential deal breaker: women who sided with the secessionist South need not have applied.

A Curious Moment in Classified History

Those already married also communicated through the notice columns. In legal notices that begin with the word *whereas*, husbands publicly disparaged their wayward wives, while revoking their power to purchase in the community. Advertisements like this one were common in the eighteenth century.

> *Buckingham townſhip, Bucks county, July 6, 1785.*
> WHEREAS my wife CHARITY has, without cauſe, eloped from my bed and board, and perſiſts in a reſolution not to live with me: Theſe are to warn all perſons not to deal with, or truſt her any thing on my account, as I ſhall not be liable to pay any debts of her contracting after this date; and whereas ſhe may be influenced to ſuch diſorderly practices, by the counſel and encouragement of ill-diſpoſed people, all perſons are hereby forewarned againſt harbouring or countenancing her in any reſpect, that ſhe may be convinced of the indecency and impropriety of her behaviour, and return to her duty. Any perſon offending againſt this notification, may expect to be dealt with as the law directs.   †   ADAM BARR.
>
> —July 13, 1785, *Pennsylvania Gazette*

Occasionally, the wife responded in a follow-up ad, contesting the charges and making a few of her own; in the case of Charity Barr, she waited a month to post a rebuttal in the newspaper.

> Buckingham townſhip, Bucks county, Auguſt 9, 1785.
> WHEREAS the ſubſcriber, Wife of ADAM BARR, much to her grief, has found her name publiſhed in the papers by her huſband, accuſing her of eloping from him without any cauſe. If being often beat and abuſed in a moſt cruel manner, thrown in the fire, ſometimes almoſt ſtrangled by him, at other times thrown on the floor and ſtamped on, ſwearing he would murder her, and other ill treatment, which diſabled her from getting out of bed for ſeveral days, ſuffering both black and white ſervants to abuſe her with ill language, and when her mother came to ſee her, he in a furious manner turned both her and her mother out of doors.----If ſuch cruel uſage, from a man who ought to have been her beſt friend, be not ſufficient cauſe for leaving him, ſhe leaves the impartial to judge.   §   CHARITY BARR.
>
> —August 10, 1785, *Pennsylvania Gazette*

A GENTLEMAN, THIRTY YEARS OF AGE, IN FULL health, possessed of ample means, well read, fond of poetry, good living and society, six-feet in his socks, dark hair and eyes, called by his intimate friends "Handsome Jones," keeps a pair of road horses, can sing, dance and play the fiddle, belongs to no club, Free Mason or Odd Fellows Association, has no idea of going to the war at present, a good whistler, and, upon the whole, a desirable person, wishes to make the acquaintance of some lady, with the ultimate view of matrimony. The lady must be plump, pleasant and pretty, not over twenty years of age (he is a great believer in the advantages of early marriage); dark complexion preferred, without curls, cotton or cosmetic; money of no account, in particular—still, some not objected to; a good dancer, without old aunts, uncles, grandmothers and grandfathers, or second, third, fourth, fifth or any other cousins (as the advertiser, although well off, cannot marry a whole family); good teeth, fond of children (the advertiser has none, however), kind to servants, domestic, chatty, clever, and well-educated. None but with good intentions need apply. Answers, with full particulars of age, size, disposition, looks, likes and dislikes, will be treated confidentially and answered, if sent to Handsome Jones, Herald office, stating when and where an interview may be had.

—February 7, 1862,
New York Herald

MATRIMONIAL—A YOUNG LADY OF GREAT beauty, and otherwise lavishly endowed ("root of all evil" included), desires to open a correspondence with a view to matrimony. She prefers this romantic method of procuring a husband. Communications strictly confidential. Address Unley Carter, box 3,275 Post office.

—February 28, 1862,
New York Herald

A YOUNG LADY, EXTRAVAGANTLY FOND OF dress, desires the acquaintance of a wealthy gentleman; no other need answer; with a view to matrimony. Address Miss Agnes Clarke, station G.

—November 24, 1865,
New York Herald

The flurry of matrimonial advertising in the mid-nineteenth century had thinned out by century's end, at least in many big city dailies. The cause for the downturn is open to speculation: perhaps the mounting bad press—scandalous stories profiling disreputable advertisers—added new stains to an already controversial practice. Matrimonial bureaus, private matchmaking services established to introduce singles to each other, *allegedly* offered a more discriminating alternative. Often these businesses pushed their own published personals, mail-order catalogs filled with "reputable" client profiles. The Select Club of Tekonsha, Michigan was one of many such companies. In 1908, the agency published "The Golden Seal Matrimonial Catalogue." It was a fifty-page pamphlet marketed directly to bachelors, with more than 250 profiles of eligible ladies from which to choose. Names were withheld, but each ad was assigned a number. For a one-dollar fee, subscribers could purchase a "key" to the catalog, a list of "the full name and address of every lady represented in this Special Matrimonial Catalogue No. 250, together with the amount of means they possess, as they have given it to us." If a courtship between two clients led to marriage, the agency collected an additional five dollars from each partner. This ad, number 39 in the catalog's line-up, was typical in form and content:

> **39**—A teacher having a kind and affectionate disposition. Who will be the first to write to me? Age 30, wt. 115, ht. 62½ ins., dark brown eyes, brunette olive skin. Welsh American, Presbyterian, highly educated musician, stylish dresser. Have had a sad life so far, but have not yet given up. I have lovely brown hair, nice teeth, good form, and eyes that my friends envy, but I am not conceited about it. Please write.

Matrimonial clubs regularly advertised their "reliable" services in a cross section of periodicals. Readers of the magazine *Hunter-Trader-Trapper*, for example, could find ads for these lonely hearts clubs; so could subscribers to the *Day*, a Yiddish newspaper published in New York City, which ran inserts for "modern matrimonial bureaus," companies with names like Samuel's, Bessie's, Evelyn's, Pauline's, Adler's, and Horne & Singer.

The newspaper personal advertisement hovered under the radar screen until the 1960s and '70s, when it attracted a new audience and found a firmer platform to stand on. It was the sexual revolution and Americans were looking for creative ways to connect. New York City's *Village Voice*, established in 1955 as the country's first and largest alternative weekly, offered a forum for these newly inspired ads:

SHY INHIBITED HARVARD STUDENT TOO MUCH INTO BOOKS, WISHES TO MEET SPONTANEOUS PERSON TO LIBERATE HIM. BOX 1933 V.V. 80 UNIV PL NY 10003.

—July 29, 1971, *Village Voice*

Single male 27, with diverse interests seeks earthy, attractive female to share life's pleasures in mutual, non-sexist framework.

—July 25, 1974, *Village Voice*

In the last few decades, personal advertising has enjoyed a rush of interest and activity. The stigma, it seems, is *finally* lifting. A new language of abbreviations has evolved, one intricate enough to warrant a regularly updated translation key (PA = photograph appreciated; SD = social drinker; SAM = single Asian male). Thousands of specialized websites try to keep up with this fast-growing market, classifying ads by nationality, geography, age group (teens to seniors), sexual preference, religious affiliation, political leaning, hobby, career, exercise habits, eating preferences, even medical condition. There are sites designed to bring together single parents, military personnel, horse lovers, or vegans looking for other "raw foodies" to date. And while plenty of advertisers still seek that old-fashioned "view to matrimony," the personals can also accommodate the search for a fishing buddy or a stranger willing to fulfill a specific sexual request.

> Sneaker Trampling—Generous SWM seeks female to trample or kick me with clean sneakers.
>
> —July 9, 2002, *Village Voice*

A Curious Moment in Classified History

Some of America's earliest gay personal ads can be found in the *Hobby Directory,* a publication turned out by the International Association of Hobbyists for Men and Boys in the summer of 1946. It was a bound booklet of personal "write-ups," classified by state, and written by males hoping to share their passion for puzzles, model trains, Lincoln head pennies, Confederate paper money, stamps, military patches, and other collectibles, with "friends far and near." The directory, sold at neighborhood craft stores, evolved into a social club for gay men.

No. 583.* Metropolitan N.Y. Age 36. Single. Writer. Interests: boating and swimming, sociology, biology, history and almost everything else. Collects objets d'art and the unusual, including physical culture photos. Visits Washington and Baltimore. C.D.: members of same interests, 18-50.

—June 1951, *Hobby Directory* (South Orange, New Jersey)

A THOUSAND WORDS

MATRIMONIAL.

A YOUNG MAN, WHO OWNS TWO FARMS IN THE country and is out of debt, wants to marry some young lady who is tall, graceful, genteel, well educated, virtuous, respectable, of good figure and very handsome. Must send their daguerreotype and address to H. S. Wilson, Morristown, N. J. N. B.—The young lady must not be over twenty years old.

—January 16, 1862, *New York Herald*

Before the invention of photography, personal advertisers used words alone to paint their portraits. But the world of newspaper courtship took a dramatic turn in 1839, when a Parisian artist named Louis J.M. Daguerre announced his invention of the daguerreotype. This, the earliest form of photography to be widely available to the general public, was enthusiastically embraced in the United States, where galleries soon opened their doors to meet the needs of a growing clientele. Men and women who could afford to return one in kind, began to request photographic images from prospective suitors. In New York City, a weekend stroll down Broadway may have included a visit to one of these galleries.

The cost of a daguerreotype varied, depending on the size of the image, but they weren't cheap. In 1853, the famous photographer Mathew Brady charged two dollars for an average-sized image at his well-respected establishments on Broadway, twice as much as a typical laborer earned working on the railroad at the time. But if you shopped around, you could find the same-sized daguerreotype for half that cost or even less, although the quality, Brady pointed out, would be compromised. To compete in the marketplace, Brady offered cheaper likenesses one year later, promising to "make better pictures for from 50 cents to $1, than have ever been made before at these prices."

> WITH MANY MISGIVINGS AS TO WHETHER AN advertisement of this kind will meet with a response from any sincere young lady, the advertiser, a gentleman of moderate means ($80,000) and good appearance, takes this method of becoming acquainted with some young lady of respectability, not over twenty-two years of age, with a view to matrimony. If such a person can treat this with any sincerity, he would be pleased to correspond with her, and, if agreeable, exchange daguerreotypes before having an interview. Address Harry P. Clarendon, box 2,038 New York Post office.
>
> —February 12, 1861, *New York Herald*

For a period, the daguerreotype cornered the photographic marketplace. But soon, other processes began to compete for attention and profit: the ambrotype, the tintype, and then the albumen-print carte de visite, introduced to America from France in 1859. A small portable photographic print roughly the size of a Victorian visiting card when mounted ($2^{1}/_{2}$ by 4 inches), the carte de visite was cheap to reproduce and more accessible to the masses. It became the visual record of popular choice.

There were risks to consider before shipping off your likeness to a perfect stranger. To this end, the 1865 book *Rogues and Rogueries of New-York: A Full and Complete Exposure of All the Swindles and Rascalities Carried On or Originated In the Metropolis* addressed the perils and pitfalls of such a transaction: "You foolish girl that imagine yourself in love with 'Adonis' and answer his advertisement, beware! You are laying a snare into which, sooner or later, you will fall. Send him your *carte de visite*—and then imagine how you would feel, could you see the depraved rascal into whose custody you thoughtlessly and trustfully gave

AN ANCIENT MAIDEN, AGED SEVENTEEN, whose heart is drifting about—don't know where to anchor—desires to fall desperately in love, as she has never been in that delightful state, wishes to communicate with someone who knows how to mind everybody's business but his own, with the hope that the congeniality of our dispositions, united, may be instrumental in making the world in general at peace with one another. Address, and inclose, carte de visite, LENNIE DAVIS, Broadway Post-office. N.B. First cousin to Jeff Davis.

—December 28, 1862, *New York Sunday Mercury*

GENTLEMEN, TAKE NOTICE—I AM IN NEED OF a husband; one who is educated and respectable. I am in my nineteenth year, considered good looking, of a very lively disposition, have plenty of friends but want some one to love, to smile when I smile, when I weep shall refrain. Address (enclosing carte de visite if possible) Florence Ellison, station G, New York.

—February 18, 1864, *New York Herald*

A GENTLEMAN WORTH $50,000 DESIRES TO MARRY a woman from 18 to 30 years old, who is willing to make home happy, with a view to matrimony. Send photographs; rejected ones returned if stamp is sent. Please address, for two weeks, Geo. H. Hutchinson, box 121 Herald office.

—February 14, 1868, *New York Herald*

Matrimonial A FISHERMAN wishes to enter into matrimony with an amiable, sensible, and charitable girl. Those who are courageous enough to battle against the cares of life, brave enough to fight, and strong enough to conquer, need not apply. No information will be given until a letter, including photograph and real address, is received. Address P. COLLINGWOOD, Lock Box 5, Gloucester Post Office.

—October 22, 1869, *Cape Ann Weekly Advertiser* (Massachusetts) it, exhibiting it in bar-rooms and other vile places, boasting of how he has the original in his power. Would not the blush of shame mantle your brow, and the tremor of apprehension possess your heart? That villain has you in his clutches, and if he pleases can blast your reputation in the eyes of the world."

In spite of such melodramatic warnings, photographic portraits continued to play an active role in newspaper introductions. The Eastman Kodak company revolutionized the photographic process in the late nineteenth century, putting the portable camera in the hands of ordinary Americans—where it remains today, widely in digital format. Now the JPEG file is a click away from landing on the desktops of online daters. Personal advertising and photography have become intertwined, with image exchange a routine—even required—step in the digital courtship ritual. But although the medium has evolved, human nature remains largely unchanged: despite the sophisticated technology, a JPEG can, in the end, be as true or misleading as a handwritten notice penned in the days before the daguerreotype.

THE LEGEND OF BELLE GUNNESS

Criminal minds take to the anonymity of the personals. That danger could lurk behind a few unremarkable lines of text was confirmed by the shocking story of Belle Gunness. Born in Norway in 1858, Brynhild Paulsdatter Størset emigrated to the United States sometime in the early 1880s. She settled in the Chicago area and soon after married Mads Sorensen. Together, the couple opened a candy store, which mysteriously burned down. Belle, as she was now called, collected on the insurance policy.

Exactly where the Sorensens lived, how many times their houses burned to the ground, and whether they had biological children, became foster parents, or adoptive ones is difficult to sort out, as different writers present conflicting accounts. What is generally accepted is that over the years, five children lived with the couple and two died in infancy. The insurance company compensated Belle for both deaths. Also undisputed is the fact that Belle collected insurance benefits again when Mads Sorensen died in the summer of 1900. The date of his death—July 30—held special meaning for Belle. According to Janet Langlois, author of *Belle Gunness: The Lady Bluebeard,* it was "the one and only day that two life insurance policies with two different mutual benefit associations overlapped." Though her husband showed clear symptoms of poisoning, the family doctor linked the sudden death to a pre-existing heart condition, and deemed an autopsy unnecessary. Belle collected on her largest insurance premium yet—$8,500—and used that money to purchase a farm on McClung Road in LaPorte, Indiana, where she moved with what was left of her family: Jennie, Myrtle, and Lucy.

Belle soon married again, on April 1, 1902, to Peter Gunness. He, too, was doomed, as was his infant daughter from a previous marriage. A week after their marriage, his baby died. Gunness himself wouldn't make it through the year; Belle buried him in December after a sausage grinder "accidentally" fell on his head. The insurance company covered the loss, again.

Allegedly, Belle gave birth to their son, Philip, in the spring of 1903. Now living comfortably on her farm in LaPorte, Belle stalked her next victims in the personals. She inserted ads in various newspapers, encouraging men with money to respond. On March 21, 1908, Belle is believed to have posted this notice in the midwestern paper the *Skandinaven.*

> WANTED—A woman who owns a beauti-
> fully located and valuable farm in first class
> condition, wants a good and reliable man as partner
> in the same. Some little cash is required for which
> will be furnished first class security. Address C.H.
> Skandinaven office.*

According to the local LaPorte mail carrier, her advertisements yielded batches of letters from interested suitors. Men brought themselves and their money to LaPorte, then disappeared. When Belle's house mysteriously burned to the ground in late April of 1908, authorities unearthed ten bodies in her backyard. In the days and weeks following the fire, thousands of sightseers packed railway cars and made the pilgrimage to her property, hoping to catch sight of the temporary morgue. They brought their children with them, bought lemonade, ice cream, and peanuts from vendors set up on the grounds, and left the scene carrying souvenirs. Years later, Janet Langlois interviewed local residents about the bizarre carnival scene. Max Ford, though not there himself, recalled his parents' memories of those "Gunness Sundays": "Chicago went crazy! The newspaper reporters—all the big papers sent their reporters. Excursions went out from Chicago at special reduced rates, and carloads and trainloads of people came into LaPorte. Holidays and Sundays. It was unbelievable that people would bring basket lunches and eat on the grounds while the bodies were being dug up."

---

* Interestingly, this ad has never been found, though it is cited in numerous accounts of the Belle Gunness murders. The fact that she ensnared bachelors through the personals is uncontested, however. An original letter that Belle wrote to Andrew Helgelein, one of the men who responded to her ad, can be viewed at the LaPorte County Historical Society.

As for the whereabouts of Belle herself, that mystery was never solved. Jennie was found buried in the yard, and Myrtle, Lucy, and Philip were discovered in the fire's remains, but whether Belle died in the blaze or escaped is still unknown. A woman's body was pulled out of the ashes, but the measurements were wrong: Belle stood five feet seven inches tall and weighed roughly two hundred pounds; the body found in the ashes was considerably lighter and significantly shorter.

A man by the name of Ray Lamphere, a former handyman at the Gunness house and, at one time, Belle's lover, was initially blamed for both the fire and the murders. A witness saw him running from the scene of the blaze. In the end, the jury convicted Lamphere of arson—which he would confess to the following year before he died in prison—but not murder. Belle, he said, had killed her children and a recently hired housekeeper (which explained the unidentified female body found at the site). She also murdered a number of men she met through the personals. According to Lamphere, he had personally helped Belle bury their bodies in the backyard. He also helped her with her cover-up and escape plan, driving her to a local train station on the fateful night of the fire.

The story of Belle Gunness lingered long after those bodies were excavated from her property and the crowds of tourists had returned home. Some insisted that they spotted the serial killer in other parts of the country over the years, but those sightings were never verified. In 1931, a woman named Esther Carlson was arrested in Los Angeles. She died in prison before her identity could be officially confirmed, but many suspected that she was, indeed, Belle Gunness. Two former LaPorte residents paid a visit to the morgue and swore they saw Belle's body there.

CHANCE ENCOUNTERS

> **IF THE LADY WHO, FROM AN OMNIBUS, SMILED** on a gentleman with a bunch of bananas in his hand, as he crossed Wall street, corner of Broadway, will address X., box 6,735 Post office, she will confer a favor.
>
> —March 21, 1866, *New York Herald*

In 1867, under the pen name Mark Twain, Samuel Langhorne Clemens worked as a roving reporter for the *Daily Alta California,* a San Francisco newspaper. His travels brought him to New York, among other stops in America and abroad, where he gathered his observations into clever essays and sent them back to the West Coast for publication. In one of those dispatches, Clemens described the country's biggest metropolis as "a splendid desert—a domed and steepled solitude, where the stranger is lonely in the midst of a million of his race." In another, he couldn't help but notice how a growing number of New Yorkers tried to ease that sense of isolation: "You may sit in a New York restaurant in the morning for a few hours, and you will observe that the very first thing each man does, before ordering his breakfast, is to call for the *Herald*—and the next thing he does is to look at the top of the first column and read the 'Personals.' "

A regular and usually colorful contributor to that column was the chance encounter—type advertisement. A woman, or more often, a man, would catch sight of an attractive stranger—in a stage coach, on a ferry, sitting in a theater balcony, or perhaps just strolling down Broadway—and, interested in making an acquaintance, would subsequently publish a note to that person in the

strange red cow

newspaper. Various local papers ran such ads, but the *New York Herald* offered a consistently wide selection: on any given day, the "Personal" column might have contained a handful, or more, of these impulsive valentines.

Clemens wasn't charmed by these poetic come-ons, or by the advertisers who were compelled to publish them: "There seems to be a pack of wooden-headed louts about this town," he wrote,

---

ON WEDNESDAY AFTER-NOON A LADY WITH black silk quilted hat walked nearly side by side with a gentleman in a drab overcoat from Tenth to Fourteenth street, in Broadway. Both were annoyed by the wind and dust. Her smile has haunted him ever since. Will she send her address to Carl, Union square Post office?

—March 8, 1861

WILL THE YOUNG LADY WHO ACCIDENTALLY fell while dancing at Barnum's Museum, on Monday evening, address a note to Interested, Herald office, as a gentleman would like to make her acquaintance, if perfectly agreeable to her?

—January 22, 1862

NIBLO'S, MONDAY EVE-NING—OCCUPIED Adjoining seats in parquet; repeated pressure of arm and foot and hands met when separating. If agreeable, address Bruno, box 211 Herald office.

—July 17, 1867

"WON'T YOU LOOK IN THE HERALD TO-MORROW?" —Will the young lady to whom the above was addressed appoint an interview with the gentleman wearing eyeglasses? Adress A.B., Station D.

—December 17, 1867

BOOTH'S THEATRE, THURS-DAY EVENING, 11TH. Will the lady who met the gent's gaze through an opera glass and smiled please address, in confidence, Harry Wilton, Herald office?

—March 13, 1869

---

personals

"who fall in love with every old strumpet who smiles a flabby smile at them in a street car, and forthwith they pop a personal into the *Herald*." He ridiculed the advertisers who, at least from his perspective, acted more like beasts of prey than proper, upstanding gentlemen: "And behold, if a respectable woman dares to look at one of these by accident, or to see if he has got hind legs and a brass collar on, up comes the inevitable personal, with a lot of stuff in it about 'the lady who kindly took notice of a gentleman,' and so forth and so on, and the equally inevitable supplication for an 'interview.' Perdition catch these whelps!"

It is true: some of these postings can paint rather desperate pictures. Advertisers described passing strangers with unsettling accuracy, sometimes noting hair color, eye color, what she was wearing, what she was carrying, in which hand she was carrying it, the direction she was heading, the time of day she was heading there, the street corner she turned at, who she was walking with, and so on. A woman couldn't move through the city, it seems, without snagging the attention of any one of these free-floating admirers.

WILL THE YOUNG LADY, WITH CURLS, WEARING a straw bonnet, and I think plaid shawl, and who carried a Herald in her hand, and who came down Park row to Broadway, and down Broadway to Dey street, turning into Dey street about 11 o'clock yesterday, and who in Dey street met and spoke to a gentleman and then went into a fur store in Dey street, near Greenwich, oblige the gentleman who stood on the opposite side of Dey street, as he very much desires an acquaintance? Address T., Herald office.

—February 28, 1862

strange red cow

Women, for their part, didn't engage in this kind of advertising nearly as often as men. But there were the exceptions. Oddly enough, this mother and son team collectively posted an ad for an attractive young woman they spotted together on the street.

A N INTRODUCTION IS EARNESTLY SOLICITED OF the young lady or her friends or family, by the gentleman and his mother who stopped their carriage Friday morning to assist a young lady who had jumped from a stage she had just entered, corner 5th av. and 39th st., to rescue the old gentleman who had fallen in the roadway. The young lady is about 20 years of age and very beautiful; wears her hair in large brown waves; has rosy complexion and soft blue eyes; wore Persian gilt walking coat and muff. We desire her acquaintance and to present her in our family. Address MOTHER AND SON, Herald Uptown office.

—February 8, 1880

And this female advertiser, Lena Bigelow, placed a notice more than a year after she had met a man while traveling.

A YEAR AGO LAST SEPTEMBER OR OCTOBER TWO ladies with a child were travelling on the Hudson River cars, one of whom offered a seat to a middle aged gentleman, with light whiskers or goatee, slightly gray, who kindly pointed out to her the red leaved trees, and said he had a number of them on his place, and made himself otherwise agreeable; and when she was leaving him (ten miles this side of where he stopped) gave her a parting embrace, which she has never been able to forget. If the gentleman has any recollection of the circumstance he will greatly oblige by addressing a note to Lena Bigelow, Madison square Post office, giving some description of the lady, also name of the paper he gave her.

—January 25, 1862

---

personals

Written for all eyes to see, these messages were meant for only one. But there was always the chance that the *wrong* one, someone other than the intended, could respond to the advertisement. To avoid that embarrassing mistake, some advertisers asked for identification, a password of sorts, in return correspondence.

WILL ONE OF THE TWO LADIES WHO rode in the cars from Coney Island to Fulton Ferry, Brooklyn, Thursday, Sept. 5, be so kind as to address a note to the young hunter who presented her with a bird, stating something that was said during the passage. Address Young Hunter, station E, New York.

—September 9, 1867

FIFTH AVENUE THEATRE, THURSDAY EVENING— Will the young lady with black hair and dark eyes, wearing velvet cloak, and who sat in balcony with two gentlemen, communicate address to her admirer on the right. State color of gloves to prevent mistake. Address Orpheus, Hopper's Post office, Twelfth Street.

—April 10, 1869

It is no wonder that so many New Yorkers built their morning ritual around reading these ads: the immediacy they communicate is irresistible, even 150 years later. Each message is an intimate tableau, a series of moments preserved in time and color. Suddenly, we are sitting next to Lena Bigelow on that Hudson River car, watching those red-leaved trees rush by! Or we are standing on a corner of Fifth Avenue, witnessing this awkward exchange:

WILL THE YOUNG LADY WHO SO KINDLY OFFERed me grace, when I accidentally stepped on her dress in Fifth avenue, on Sunday last, allow me to offer any further apologies in person? If agreeable, please answer through this column, as an everlasting impression has been made on   CHARLES BYRON.

—February 11, 1862

---

strange red cow

In spite of Twain's unfavorable review, the chance encounter ad has survived the years. We know them by a variety of category headings—"Missed Connections," "I Saw You," "Caught My Eye"—but the theme is the same: these ads offer, at the very least, the hope of a second chance.

I LOVE NERDS
I not-quite met you at the Mirabeau Room on Friday, July 30, 2004 at the Bollywood party. You were with three of your guy pals (one was Persian maybe?). ME: visiting a friend in Seattle, told you I didn't live there, had on an "i love nerds" t shirt and a daisy in my hair. YOU: Indian, super nice and cute. I gave you the daisy at the end of the night and didn't even get your name or anything. haven't forgotten you and am kicking myself for not giving you my number. make contact!

When: Friday, July 30, 2004
Where: Mirabeau Room, Bollywood Party
I saw a: Man
I am a: Woman

—August 7, 2004, *The Stranger* (Seattle, Washington)

I saw you . . . i was getting searched next to the holding cell for men, when they walked a line of women by. you were barefoot, looked angry, and i can't stop thinking about you.

—December 28, 2001, *www.isawyou.com*

Whole Foods Blues, Glover Park Sunday, Sept 19. You had blue blue eyes, and light blue pedal pushers. I had black jeans and a checkered shirt. You didn't know that you were being checked-out, just as you were checking out your boullion and jam. But maybe you did know? No, I said to myself, you should be able to do your shopping in peace without the bother of gazing admirers. Alas, courteous fools like me must take our chances in the City Paper!

—September 19, 2004, *Washington City Paper* (Washington, D.C.)

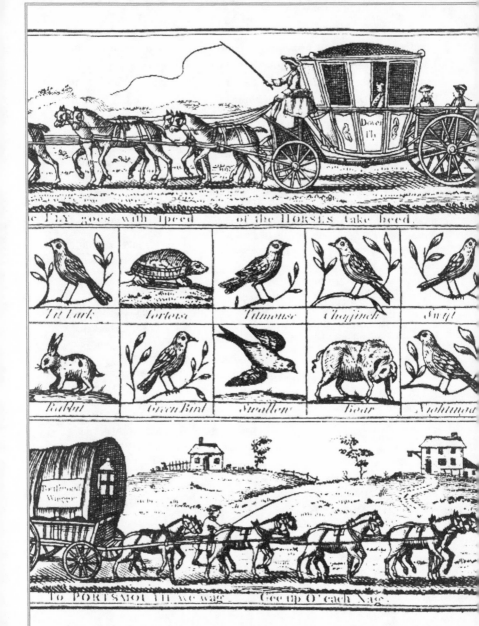

e FLY goes with speed   of the HORSES take heed.

Tit Lark	Tortoise	Titmouse	Chaffinch	Snipt
Rabbit	Green Bird	Swallow	Boar	Nightingale

To PORTSMOUTH we wag   Gee up O'each Nag.

CHAPTER 5

Help Wanted

> **WW**ANTED—A young lady of German parentage; must be a 36 bust and understand bookkeeping on a small scale. Apply Milbauer & Bleiweiss, ladies' and misses' cloaks, 419 Broadway.
>
> —January 2, 1892, *New York World*

The help-wanted section was one of the fastest growing classified categories in the last half of the nineteenth century. As millions of immigrants moved to the United States—more than 37 million poured into American ports between 1820 and 1930—the simultaneous need for work on the part of the newcomers and the need for laborers on the part of an industrializing nation caused an explosion of job-related advertising. Large-scale construction projects—canal digging, bridge building, the laying of over two hundred thousand miles of railroad track—demanded large-scale recruitment efforts. For the immigrant with both the desire and the desperate economic need to make a living in a new land, the classifieds provided a regularly up-dated list of options out there. Work-related listings included notices posted by employers seeking reliable help, but the section also made room for situation-wanted ads, inserts placed by the other half—the worker—in search of just about every kind of opportunity.

WANTED IMMEDIATELY, 100 HANDS, To work upon the NEW PHILADELPHIA, LATERAL CANAL $12 PER MONTH will be given. APPLY TO MATTHEW STUART. New Philad. Aug 18, 1835.

—October 6, 1835, *Tuscarawas Advocate* (Ohio)

WANTED—A SITUATION IN A JEW FAMILY, AS Housekeeper or Cook, by a very respectable, well recommended, tidy young Jewess, who has been in this country five years, and can give the best of city references as to character and respectability; is a first rate cook, and speaks English fluently. Please call at 191½ Bowery.

—May 13, 1852, *New York Herald*

WANTED, 200 LABORERS, to work on Sections 1, 2, & 12, Virginia Central Railroad. Wages one dollar per day; but if you are disposed to make sectional distinctions or quarrels, you need not come, for you cannot stay on my work.
MICHAEL O'BRIEN, Contractor

—January 29, 1853, *Boston Pilot*

WANTED — A COOK, WASHER AND IRONER; ONE who perfectly understands her business; any color or country except Irish. Apply at 69 East Fourteenth, between the hours of 9 and 11.

—May 13, 1853, *New York Herald*

Immigrants were more likely to work for less and plenty of employers recruited directly from those communities; others openly favored native-born, "American" candidates.

> **A** FIRST-CLASS CARPENTER wanted, of about 25 years of age, having some experience with wood-working machinery; must be an American, of American parentage, a Protestant, and a graduate of public school; must be naturally handy with a pen, quick and correct at figures; a good opportunity and a permanent position for a bright, active young man of the right sort. Address, stating particulars, E.B.J., Boston Transcript.
>
> —June 23, 1897, *Boston Evening Transcript*

Job requirements have evolved over the years, and so has the language once used to describe the labor market's "ideal" candidates. What positions were offered to which sex, what opportunities were reserved for which racial group or religious affiliation, who was considered young or fit enough, or too old to get the job done—are issues that have long played out in the work place and the notice columns of the newspaper.

> **W**anted—A intelligent, lame lad is wanted in this office as an apprentice. He must be intelligent, as we do not expect such to join the "secesh," and we would like it very much if he were a cripple so there would be no danger of his enlisting in Uncle Sam's army—Whoever is selected will in consideration of his being a cripple, be paid in United States money. All other will be paid Secession scrip.
>
> —November 9, 1861, *Stars & Stripes*
> (Bloomfield, Missouri)

BOY—Wanted, colored boy not over 4½ feet in height to do office work; $3 per week. C., box 182 World.

—June 21, 1892, *New York World*

NEGRO SHOE MAKERS WANTED Fifty Negro SHOE-MAKERS wanted at once, at the Confederate States Shoe Manufac-tory. In this place, I will pay from $150 to $200, according to capacity. All able-bodied soldiers are needed at the front, hence this appeal to negro shoemakers.

L.O. BRIDEWELL
Major in charge.

—January 1, 1865, *Daily Chronicle & Sentinel* (Georgia)

Over time, discrimination in the workplace—recruiting a specific group or excluding one—became increasingly more controversial. "It is general practice to prohibit mention of specific ages in offers of employment for women, although such necessary qualifications as 'under 30,' 'middle age,' etc., are acceptable," was the edict put forth in Morton McDonald's 1936 resource guide, *Getting and Keeping Classified Advertising.* Just a few years later, this female advertiser voiced her frustration with a system that discounted her abilities based on her age.

NO ONE seems to want a nurse who is 50 years old. I've 24 yrs.' experience in all kinds nursing, can cook, keep house, drive a car, make quilts, knit — yes, milk cows and make butter. I'm discouraged . . . because I know there's "lots of life in this old gal yet." JF411

—February 1940, *Yankee* (Dublin, New Hampshire)

On the subject of racial prejudice, McDonald offered this murky advice: "There is scarcely a paper in America that does not prohibit mention of the phrases 'no Filipinos' or 'Mohammedans' in its advertising. The barring of a race or a creed implies prejudice and promptly arouses it. . . . On the other hand, an inclusive restriction such as 'Mohammedans only,' by expressing a preference, implies a compliment and is therefore never rejected."

> WANTED: White Waitress, Waganer's Cafe, Fairhope Ave. 24-1t-p
> —January 23, 1941, *Fairhope Courier* (Alabama)

More than two decades after Wagner's Café sought a "white waitress" in the newspaper, Congress formally addressed discriminatory hiring practices. The Civil Rights Act of 1964, which protected voting rights, banned discrimination in public facilities, and prohibited employment discrimination based on race, color, religion, sex, or national origin, is considered the most important American civil rights legislation since post–Civil War Reconstruction. Laws addressing age discrimination followed three years later, and in 1990, Congress passed the Americans with Disabilities Act. Though true equality in the workplace is far from fully realized, the legal framework is in place—and tested regularly—to ensure those rights. Today, the phrase *Equal Opportunity Employer* is recognized by its abbreviation, E.O.E, now an entry in the dictionary and a standard trademark of help-wanted advertising.

LARGE FAMILIES WANTED

> ## LABOURERS.
>
> WANTED, at the Old Cotton Mill in Pawtucket, two or three Families of Children, and several young Women, to work in the Factory, to whom good Wages will be given, and constant Employ. Enquire of SAMUEL SLATER, at Pawtucket, or of ALMY and BROWN.
>
> *Providence, 3 Mo. 4, 1808.*
>
> —March 5, 1808, *Providence Gazette*

American textile manufacturing turned out its first product—cotton yarn—in the town of Pawtucket, Rhode Island. In 1790, a mill began operation there, the first in North America to use mechanized spinning technology in a factory setting. The mastermind behind the mill's success was an English mechanic named Samuel Slater, who shared his extensive knowledge of British textile production with the firm, Almy & Brown of Providence, Rhode Island, and together the partners launched the nation's textile industry.

At first, the mill employed local children—as young as seven, as old as fourteen—without the need for help-wanted notices. By week four of the operation, nine children worked there—seven boys, two girls—earning between $.80 and $1.40 per week. At the time, hiring child labor was not the moral dilemma it would later become, but a practical, economic choice: the hands of a child could navigate the mechanical parts more easily than an adult's at a much cheaper rate. Youngsters long used to working on the family farm or serving as apprentices to artisans now took their place as wage earners on the factory floor.

By 1809, dozens of cotton mills were up and running or in the process of being built in New England; many more would dot the landscape in the following decades. The pool of local workers couldn't satisfy the needs of the growing industry. To deal with the chronic labor shortage, manufacturers built mill villages, and hired families with large numbers of children to live and work there. The recruitment of the family unit became a signature of the Rhode Island factory system, as did the concept of on-site tenement housing and the requisite company store, where wages often functioned as credit and helped finance the household shopping list: meat, shoes, thread, ginger, tea, rum, etc. Though some families migrated to these mill towns unsolicited in search of opportunity, others must have made the journey after spotting an advertisement in the *Massachusetts Spy,* the *Providence Gazette,* and other New England newspapers.

WANTED
At the Bennington Cotton Factory,
SEVERAL FAMILIES that can furnish a number of children each. To such constant employ will be given, and wages paid according to the ability of the children, by

BENJAMIN PECK.
10th Month, 13, 1821

—October 30, 1821, *Vermont Gazette*

For a struggling New England family, the mill village offered clear incentives. With three or four children simultaneously employed in the factory, the collective weekly earnings mounted. And tenement housing, though not free, kept families together. The

EMPLOYMENT WANTED, two or three FAMILIES, with Children, Males or Females, from 7 to 18 Years of Age, to whom constant Employment will be given. Suitable Tenements, at moderate Rents, can be provided. For further Particulars enquire at this Office.

—July 13, 1805,
Providence Gazette

FAMILIES WANTED THREE or four Families with Children will meet with constant Employment and good Wages at the HOPE COTTON FACTORY, in Scituate. Also wanted, a good MULE SPINNER,* or a young Man to learn to spin upon a Mule. Apply at the said Factory, or to the Subscriber, in Providence.

THOMAS S. WEBB, Agent.

—July 7, 1810,
Providence Gazette

WANTED, At the Factory of LELAND MORSE & Co., two or three FAMILIES, of four or five Children each. Those who are in the habit of profanity or Sabbath breaking, and intend to continue these practices, are invited not to make application.

They also want a few hundred thousand yards of extra fine STRAW BRAID, in exchange for English, India, and Domestick Goods.

—March 8, 1820, *Massachusetts Spy,
or Worcester Gazette*

WANTED, At SAMUEL SLATER'S Factory, in Oxford—a MASTER-FARMER, to take the lead of three or four men. One with a family, to work in the Mill, would be preferred.— *Also*, wanted, a common LABOURING MAN, with a large family, to work in the Mill. Good recommendations will be required as to industry, temperance, &c. Apply at the Mill. Oxford, March 29, 1820

—March 29, 1820, *Massachusetts Spy,
or Worcester Gazette*

---

* A mule spinner operates a machine called a mule, which draws and twists fiber into thread or yarn, and then winds it onto a spool.

cost of rent was affordable, often cheaper than accomodations found elsewhere. In 1815, William Davis, his wife, and seven children moved into factory-owned tenements at the Slater-Tiffany Mill in Massachusetts. According to the company's account books, rent cost the Davis's roughly 7 percent of the collective family income in 1821, an expense fully covered by the salary pulled in by nine-year-old Ruth that year.

Still, there was plenty to complain about. Work was inconsistent and layoffs routine. In 1827, the Slater-Tiffany mill downsized significantly, letting go of the entire Davis family. Even during periods of active employment, payment was erratic. In some factories, manufacturers compensated their workers quarterly; others, only twice a year. Those who paid regularly in cash considered the practice a benefit worth emphasizing.

HELP WANTED,

AT the Cotton Factories of Samuel Slater, at South Oxford, in the different branches of the Cotton Manufacturing Business, for one year from the first day of April next, for which liberal wages will be paid in CASH, *every two weeks*. A few good Families, furnishing help in the different departments, would meet with good encouragement. Also, Overseers and Mule Spinners would do well to call. None need apply who cannot come well recommended for *faithfulness* and *sobriety*.

South Oxford, Feb. 13.   4w

—February 13, 1828, *Massachusetts Spy, and Worcester County Advertiser*

Once inside the factory, employees faced a hostile work environment. The six-day work week—beginning each morning before sunrise and ending after dusk—took its toll on the body and mind, and the relentless rotation of machinery mangled arms, hands, scalps. The monotony of those long hours could be interrupted at any moment by a sudden and serious injury. Poor ventilation, flurries of airborne lint, dim lighting, and frigid temperatures during the colder months all jeopardized the health of mill workers. It's no wonder that these families pursued better environments whenever they could find them.

Wanted.

A T the Albion Mills, SIX good Families of Weavers Spinners and Carding Room help. Better Tenements, and warmer Factories cannot be found at any village. Fair wages will be given. Any persons wishing for such a situation, will enquire at the Mills, or of GEO. WILKINSON.

—January 11, 1833, *Pawtucket Chronicle and Rhode-Island and Massachusetts Register*

The profile of the village mill worker would change over the nineteenth century. Large New England families, once recruited so aggressively in the newspaper, eventually left the textile mills behind. As they became increasingly less tolerant of the factory conditions, immigrants from Ireland, Canada, and other countries—determined to earn a living in the United States no matter the abuses—arrived in waves, ready to serve as their replacements.

A Curious Moment in Classified History

After the power loom was introduced to America in 1814, mills could turn raw bales of cotton into finished pieces of cloth in one location. Large-scale factories—the mills of Lowell, Massachusetts, and Exeter, New Hampshire, for example—embraced the power loom technology, and hired young Yankee women—not children—to operate those machines. Newspaper advertising, however, was generally *not* used to recruit them. Convincing a young, single woman to move from her family home to a factory boardinghouse required more than a few generic lines of print in the newspaper. Instead, agents traveled to neighboring states to personally enlist a female workforce. This ad is one of the exceptions.

Weavers Wanted.

GOOD encouragement will be given to a number of smart GIRLS to attend Power Looms in the Exeter Cotton Manufactory. Those acquainted with Weaving would be preferred. Apply to the Superintendant at the Factory, or to the subscriber.
JOHN ROGERS, Agent.
Exeter, Dec. 6, 1823.   6w

—January 3, 1824, *Portsmouth Journal of Literature and Politics* (New Hampshire)

FRESH BREAST OF MILK

WANTED—A WET NURSE, FOR A CHILD THREE months old, to go a short distance in the country; one having lost her child preferred. Apply to R. Cooper, M. D., 346 1st av.

—August 1, 1861, *New York Herald*

In the eighteenth and nineteenth centuries, the medical community, religious leaders, and various social advice givers considered the act of breast-feeding a "sacred office," and strongly encouraged women to breast-feed their infants whenever possible. But not every mother could fulfill that office. A sick woman, too weak to breast-feed, needed to find another way to sustain her baby. And when a woman died during childbirth, and her baby survived, a viable feeding alternative needed to be secured, and promptly.

A baby in need of sustenance could be hand-fed, but for years, that option presented worrisome complications: the artificial foods available (the milk of an animal, sometimes mixed with flour, water, or sugar) were harder to digest than human breast milk, and the feeding implements were clumsy and inefficient, hampering the flow of food to the baby. Though not known at the time, those utensils also harbored dangerous bacteria when not properly cleaned. Moreover, in the days before refrigeration, keeping artificial foods fresh posed an ongoing challenge. Simply put, babies fed by the breast, not the bottle, were more likely to survive. Thus, for years a good breast of milk was considered a valuable professional resource, sought and peddled openly in the notice columns of American newspapers.

> WANTED, A YOUNG HEALTHY WET NURSE. One who has had the smallpox will be most agreeable.—Inquire of the printer.
>
> —February 21, 1765, *Georgia Gazette*

> WANTED, a Wet Nurse—a white woman preferred. Apply at the corner of Broad and 2d streets, to
> ROBERT RYAN.
>
> —February 22, 1853, *Daily Dispatch* (Richmond, Virginia)

> WET NURSE WANTED—ONE WHO IS TEMPERATE, honest, young, and healthy. Reference required. Apply at 429 5th av., corner 41st st.
>
> —May 16, 1861, *New York Herald*

> WANTED—A WOMAN TO WETNURSE A CHILD AT her own residence; one having lost her own child preferred; reference required. Apply at 31 West 35th st., to-day.
>
> —December 18, 1865, *New York Herald*

Qualified candidates, their breasts full of milk, need not have waited patiently until a "wet nurse wanted" posting spontaneously surfaced in the local newspaper. After losing their own babies, this woman and others rushed to advertise their time-sensitive services.

> WET NURSE—A RESPECTABLE married lady, having lost her baby, wishes to engage as WET NURSE. Best reference. Apply at 253 Kearny, between Pacific and Broadway.
>
> —January 7, 1859, *Daily Alta* (San Francisco, California)

A MARRIED WOMAN, with a good Breast of Milk, who has lately lost her Child, wishes to take one to suckle. Apply to JOSEPH WEST, Rehoboth, three miles from India Bridge, on the Post-Road to Warren.

—April 7, 1809, *American*
(Rhode Island)

A HEALTHY YOUNG WOMAN, WITH A FRESH breast of milk, who has lost her own baby, two months old, wishes a situation as nurse in a respectable family, or to take a child at her own residence. Call at 24 Thames st., near Trinity church.

—August 1, 1861,
New York Herald

WANTED—BY A YOUNG WOMAN, WITH A FRESH breast of milk, a child to nurse at her own place—has no child, as her own died. Good city reference given, and city reference required. Can be seen at 26 Whitehall street.

—June 4, 1852, *New York Herald*

WET NURSE—A YOUNG MARRIED ENGLISH WOMAN, whose baby is four months' old, wants a situation in a gentleman's family. None other need apply at 489 2d av., between 30th and 31st sts., first floor, front.

—January 16, 1862, *New York Herald*

The fact that these women had suffered the loss of their own infants may have worked for them in the pursuit of a job, or against them. With no child of her own to nurse, a grieving mother could provide another woman's infant her undivided attention, and her complete milk supply.

But some employers would hire only mothers with healthy infants at home, even demanding that a candidate bring along her baby to the interview. In *A Social History of Wet Nursing in America*, Janet Golden explains: "Careful inspection of the infant helped to rule out the presence of a communicable disease, provided evidence that the woman gave milk capable of nourishing a child, and allowed prospective employers to see if the wet nurse's infant was close in age to the suckling. Many doctors believed that young infants could not consume "old milk," commonly defined as having come from women who had nursed for six months or more." But inspecting a candidate's baby was not a foolproof test: if a woman needed work badly enough, she could temporarily borrow another woman's child—from a relative, friend, or neighbor—just for the sake of the interview.

WANTED — A WET NURSE — A HEALTHY WOMAN WITH a fresh breast of milk—she should bring her child. Apply at No. 797 Broadway, on Monday and Tuesday mornings, before 11 o'clock.

—March 18, 1849, *New York Herald*

A "fresh breast of milk" was a key factor, and advertisers regularly inserted that phrase into their notices. Other criteria appeared as well: "respectable," "married," "healthy," "temperate," "neat," "clean," "responsible"—language used both by the wet nurses marketing their services and the families who sought to secure them. The profession attracted poor, single women (often those who had given birth out of wedlock), and the words punctuating these advertisements spoke to a growing set of cultural anxieties about the character of those women. By the late nineteenth century, concerns about disease, the moral makeup of the wet nurse, and the fear that she could pass down sickness as well as undesirable psychological traits to a baby through her breast milk (all long-debated topics) got louder and harder to ignore.

Meanwhile, new and improved artificial feeding alternatives, including doctor-approved infant formulas, became available, first in Europe, then in America. In 1869, stores in the United States began to sell Liebig's Soluble Food for one dollar, a formula conceived by the German chemist Justus von Liebig. "No More Wet Nurses!" proclaimed one of the company's advertisements, which appeared in the magazine *Hearth & Home*. In the 1870s, Henri Nestlé, a Swiss businessman and founder of the now famous Nestlé Company, introduced his formula to the American market, a cocktail of malt, cow's milk, sugar, and wheat flour, available for fifty cents a bottle. By the late-nineteenth century, the Sears, Roebuck Company was promoting a handful of formula brands in its catalog pages, including Mellin's Infant Food and Horlick's Malted Milk.

Bottle-feeding replaced, in great part, the need for wet nurses. The popular view, including the advice of the medical community, still encouraged mothers to breast-feed their babies, but formula, *no longer* the breast of a wet nurse, became the next best option. The notice columns in the newspaper reflect this shift: in 1857 the *Philadelphia Public Ledger* printed 358 advertisements for wet nurses (posted by families, wet nurses themselves, and agencies); forty years later, at century's end, only 14 could be spotted in the pages of that paper. A wet nurse could still find employment in the early decades of the twentieth century, in hospitals and orphanages, but her role in the private home had diminished noticeably.

A PLAIN, ROUND HAND

In the mid-nineteenth century, a busy legal practice would have needed at least one copyist on staff, someone with clear handwriting who could meticulously duplicate documents by hand, and then proofread his work for overlooked errors. Writing schools offered classes in penmanship, and self-instruction manuals encouraged students to develop the skill by practicing copying. In the *Gentlemens' Writing Book,* male readers were instructed to transcribe short telling statements, among them: "A neat handwriting is a letter of recommendation." Indeed, good penmanship, along with accurate spelling and grammar, was once its own job referral, a passport for men into the mercantile world. Even the job of an office or errand boy typically required a neat hand. Clear writing, beyond its power to communicate, heralded a decent and dependable individual, one, simply put, worth hiring.

Before and during the Civil War, men filled the majority of office jobs. Many entered the field as office boys, and worked their way up. But in the last quarter of the nineteenth century, the gender makeup began to change. As commerce grew alongside industrialization, there was simply more paperwork to process daily, and the need for clerical help mounted. It was around this time that the typewriter was introduced as a time-saving mechanism. Various inventors had tried perfecting an efficient "writing machine" as early as 1714, but it wasn't until 1868 that Christopher Latham Sholes of Wisconsin came up with a viable working model. Over the next few years, Sholes and several collaborators made improvements to that model, and by 1874, E. Remington and Sons was manufacturing it. Businesses eventually invested widely in the time-saving mechanism and valued workers who could master it. An increasing number of those workers were women. A typist and stenographer could accomplish the tasks previously delegated to a copyist at a more reliable and rapid rate, but the skill of penmanship did not, in the face of this new technology, go suddenly obsolete.

A YOUNG WOMAN wanted for six weeks to address envelopes; one who can write the vertical hand found in "The Natural System of Vertical Writing," published by D.C. Heath & Co. Address, in own handwriting, P.O. Box 5164, Boston.

—September 11, 1897, *Boston Evening Transcript*

T YPEWRITER—Intelligent stenographer and typewriter; must spell correctly, write a good hand and furnish own machine; salary to begin $7 a week; address in own handwriting, also sample of typewriting. M.L. bost 237 World.

—January 17, 1892, *New York World*

B OOKKEEPER— Recommended lady, with nice handwriting who is accurate in figuring and typewriting (Remington), find steady position; state salary expected and give references. S.S. 524 Herald Downtown.

—August 5, 1909, *New York Herald*

S TENOGRAPHER and typewriter—Good penman can advance to good position as private secretary; no pay first month or two. Lock box 513, 120 Broadway.

—January 19, 1892, *New York World*

In the first half of the twentieth century, job listings for office workers, especially bookkeepers, sporadically asked candidates to respond in "own handwriting," but the invention of new office technology—the copy machine in the 1960s, the personal computer in the 1970s—would eventually pave over those lingering requests. "A plain, round hand," once a telltale sign of good character, lost its widespread currency; it matters little in an office culture now dependent on the skilled navigation of the latest computer software programs.

Saucepan	Pitcher	Footman	Trunk	Mouse trap
Flower Drudger	Table	Box Iron	Tea kettle	Butter Boat
Gridiron	Basket	Bowl of Punch	Pair of Pattens	Wig
Nursing Lamp	Shovel & Rake	Pepper Box & Spoon	Ink Stand	Bath Stove
Hat	Decanter	Tea Pot	Mug	Horn
Horse-shoes	Watchmans Rattle	Candlestick & Snuffers	Salt Box	Hammer & Chisel
Porridge Pot	Spectacles	Desk	Cannon	Music Book

CHAPTER 6

Swap

> ### 5B—SWAP THIS FOR THAT
> WILL trade new tenor banjo for payment on car. Phone Mr. Shaw, nights, 5-3600.
>
> —September 16, 1932, *Florida Times-Union*
> (Jacksonville)

The word *swap* comes from *swappen,* the Middle English verb meaning "to strike," as in striking hands in closing a business deal. In the case of a swap, that deal is a voluntary exchange of goods or services for other goods or services, without the use of money. In colonial America, lumber, tobacco, corn, livestock, nails, bullets, animal pelts, and wampum were among the currencies that passed hands in a trade. The "purchase" of Manhattan in 1626 was supposedly a swap: Dutch colonists didn't buy the island from the Native Americans for twenty-four dollars, as legend has it, but traded the land for sixty guilders' worth of goods. No bill of sale has survived, so we don't know the terms of the transaction, or which items, or how many of them, paid for the real estate deal, but perhaps they were similar to the list of goods exchanged for Staten Island: agricultural tools, kettles, and other practical wares.

By the time the first classified advertisement appeared in an American newspaper in the spring of 1704, swapping was a well-established tradition: colonial-era textbooks devoted entire chapters to the subject of bartering; ministers and schoolteachers collected their pay in produce; taxes could be paid in grain; store-keepers traded new merchandise for farm-fresh food; parcels of land could be purchased with pork, butter, cheese, anything deemed valuable enough by the seller and buyer alike.

COWDERY & DUTTON, WANTED, in exchange for their work, most kinds of LUMBER, such as Birch, Maple, Pine and Hemlock Scantling; Birch, Pine and Hemlock, (inch and half inch) Boards; Pine and Hemlock Planks—Also, Produce of all kinds, and a few Cords of Fire Wood, for which the highest price will be paid.

—November 8, 1833, *Vermont Republican & Journal*

SAVE YOUR ASHES "A penny saved is a penny made." WE will pay in trade the highest market price for *Good house and field Ashes,** delivered at our Ashery in Dover.

LEE & SCOTT.

—September 29, 1835, *Tuscarawas Advocate* (Ohio)

---

* An ashery converted hardwood ash into a product called potash, a key ingredient used to make many eighteenth- and nineteenth-century supplies, including glass, soap, and paper. These businesses burned down trees to generate ash, but they also relied on a supply from local residents.

A VELOCIPEDE* WANTED—
IN EXCHANGE FOR dentistry; for one in perfect order first class work will be guaranteed. Address Dentist, Herald office.

—April 22, 1869,
New York Herald

WANTED.
To trade fine city and ranch property in and near the city of Phenix; for cattle. Address H.B. St. Claire.
Phenix, A.T.

—February 24, 1887, *Hoof and Horn*
(Prescott, Arizona)

SINGER OR DOMESTIC
I want to exchange a Sewing Machine for a cheap boat, one suitable for a trip up Salt River in November. Also one for a second hand grocery wagon, and wanted to buy a light pair of wheels with pole for truck wagon.
AH SIN, North Hope, Me.

—October 18, 1892, *Rockland Courier-Gazette* (Maine)

WANTED.
To exchange new sewing machine or furniture for good young Jersey cow.

A.C. BRADBURY, Newport, Me.

—April 16, 1896, *Pittsfield Advertiser* (Maine)

* A velocipede (Latin for "fast feet") was an early wooden bicycle also known as the "bone shaker" for its rough ride.

FREE PRESS

Newspaper publishers personally took advantage of the swap format to announce their desire to trade subscription and advertising fees for any number of practical items. Subscribers could settle their accounts at the office with perishable provisions or durable goods. That subscribers often settled their debts late, or sometimes not at all, is evident by the frequency, and tenor, of publishers' repeated pleas in the newspaper.

Those persons who take this paper, and engaged to pay me in Rye, Indian-Corn, Butter, Cheese, Sheep's Wool, Wood, &c. are requested to make payment, as I am in want of these articles.

ISAIAH THOMAS

—May 4, 1789,
Massachusetts Spy

Such Subscribers to this Gazette as have contracted to make Payment in Wood, Grain, or other Articles of Country Produce, are requested to perform their Engagements.

—September 29, 1792,
*Providence Gazette
and Country Journal*

40 lbs. of Geese Feathers, WILL be taken in payment for News-papers, Advertisements or Books, at the office of the Vermont Gazette, if delivered soon.

—January 14, 1817,
Vermont Gazette

When publishers weren't chasing down overdue accounts, many of them, it seems, were rounding up enough rags to keep their newspapers in print. Boiled down in paper mills, pressed through rollers, and laid flat to dry, those linen and cotton rags became the physical paper on which the news was printed. A chronic shortage of rags during the Revolutionary War, and through much of the nineteenth century, prompted paper mills and publishers to ask for assistance from their communities.

These piecemeal contributions made a difference, no doubt, but American paper mills required a far greater supply. By the mid-nineteenth century, the United States was turning out more newspapers than any other nation in the world—over 2,500 titles in 1850. Rags from abroad made publishing so many pages of

R A G S.

IT is earneſtly requeſted that the fair Daughters of Liberty in this extenſive County would not neglect to ſerve their country, by ſaving for the Paper-Mill in Sutton, all Linen and Cotton and Linen Rags, be they ever ſo ſmall, as they are equally good for the purpoſe of making paper, as thoſe that are larger. A bag hung up at one corner of a room, would be the means of ſaving many which would be otherwiſe loſt. If the Ladies ſhould not make a fortune by this piece of œconomy, they will at leaſt have the ſatiſfaction of knowing they are doing an eſſential ſervice to the community, which with EIGHT PENCE per pound, the price now given for clean white rags, they muſt be ſenſible will be a ſufficient regard.

—November 26, 1778, *Massachusetts Spy or, American Oracle of Liberty*

RAGS WANTED.
American Preceptors,
School Bibles, on fine paper,
Webster's American Spelling Book,
Writing and Letter Paper,

WILL be given for clean LINEN or COTTON RAGS, at four cents per pound, at the Office of the *Western Spy & Literary Cadet*. No. 108, Main street. ‥
Cincinnati, May, 18°1

—November 10, 1821, *Western Spy & Literary Cadet*

RAGS.
Writing paper and Books given in exchange for Cotton or Cotton and Linen Rags at this office.

—May 4, 1822, *Kennebec Gazette* (Maine)

newsprint feasible. (Italy exported the largest share: 24 million pounds' worth in 1854 alone.) Over time, however, the high cost and limited supply of rag paper forced the newspaper industry to print on sheets of more cost-effective and plentiful wood-pulp paper instead. The transition from rag to wood took place gradually. On June 22, 1870, the *New York World* reported that its paper was made from a blend of raw materials, two-fifths wood pulp and three-fifths rag. By the 1880s, most newspapers were choosing wood pulp over rag, and requests to swap cotton and linen scraps, once voiced in the newspaper, quieted.

swap

Down and Out

When an economy weakens, people organically fall back on the age-old system of trade. After the American stock market crashed in 1929, a bartering fever seized the nation. Cash was scarce and swapping food, services, and other valuables became a popular way of coping with the crisis.

> ## 5B—SWAP THIS FOR THAT
> WILL exchange $450 equity Chevrolet Special Sedan, like new for equity in modern bungalow or for year's rent of same. See car at 508 West 18th st. mornings.
>
> —September 25, 1932, *Sunday Times-Union*
> (Jacksonville, Florida)

Local bartering groups were mobilized, making it easier for Americans to trade their skills and commodities with one another. The first Depression-era "self-help" organization took root in Seattle, Washington. There, in the summer of 1931, the Unemployed Citizens' League was organized. By the end of that year, twelve thousand members had joined that barter effort. The movement spread south to California, where it thrived, the climate warm and consistent enough to yield a year-round supply of agricultural crops for ready exchange. Similar groups sprung up in other regions of the country. In Salt Lake City, Utah, the National Development Association formed in the fall of 1931 and, within a year, recruited thirty thousand participants. An article from March of 1933 printed in the *Nation* counted 159 barter groups in 127 cities of 29 American states. A cross section of periodicals, from banking magazines to public health journals to mainstream city newspapers, profiled stories about these various bartering efforts.

In Virginia, a barter exchange set up between the Roanoke County school district and the nearby hospitals made it possible to trade food for medical care. Schoolchildren donated what they could daily—"a fresh, sound egg, apple or potato," for example—and over a two-month period in the winter of 1933, managed to accrue "210 pounds of chicken, 100 bushels of potatoes, 895 dozen eggs, and 310 quarts of canned fruit." In exchange for that food supply, surgeons at the local hospitals performed operations on eighteen local schoolchildren too poor to otherwise afford medical care. Not far away, in Abington, Virginia, the Barter Theatre opened its doors and traded foodstuff for performance tickets. Forty cents was the price of admission in the summer of 1933, or the equivalent in pickles, vegetables, a fresh cut of meat, home-baked cakes, or anything else a customer felt compelled to bring to the ticket booth that day.

Although Franklin Delano Roosevelt introduced the New Deal in 1933, it would take a full decade and heavy defense spending to get America back on her feet. It was in the midst of this economic climate that *Yankee* magazine, a New Hampshire—based monthly, devoted an entire column to the world of "swopping." Beginning in December of 1935, anyone with "anything genuine to swop" was invited to use the classified service for free. Each month, thrifty-minded New England folk took up the offer. In less than a year, the popularity of the "Swopper's Column" moved it from the back pages of the magazine to the front.

One mandolin, with all its strings, dulcet tone for basket of vegetables.

—December 1935

To Swop: 1 Funk & Wagnall's Standard Desk Dictionary for lightish sledge hammer or dung fork in fair condition.

—November 1936

Two books fine condition: *Woman, Her Sex and Love Life*, and *Birth Control*, by eminent physician, valuable to newly-wed couple or ones about to be united. Will swop for ten hens of heavy breed or pigs.

—June 1937

Large bell wanted. Suitable to attach to farm house and loud enough to be heard in the fields. What do you want for it?

—July 1937

I've a dandy wooden cider-press about a hundred years old which makes a bucketfull at one pressing. It's yours for four gallons of first quality white outside house paint.

—August 1937

Wistful bachelor will swop 6 pairs holey wool socks (swell for rugs) for 2 pairs wholey ones.

—November 1937

I'm a farmer, and the heavy black U.S. rubber raincoat size 38 which I bought last summer, scares my calves when I'm trying to catch them in a storm. Will swop raincoat, used but little, for what have you.

—October 1938

The role of barter shifted after World War Two as the country regained its financial balance. No longer an urgent practice, it still attracted loyal participants, as it probably always will, so long as people have something to give up for something they hope to gain. The swap system flourished as a smart, economical practice, even during prosperous times. The "Swopper's Column" survives today, online and on paper, and is considered the oldest barter column in the country.

strange red cow

THE SUBURBAN TRADING POST

Constructed and named after the home building firm Levitt and Sons, the community of Levittown, New York, provided instant, affordable housing to some of the sixteen million soldiers returning home from service in Europe, the Pacific, and on army bases stateside after World War Two. Many had marriage and children on their minds, but the postwar housing shortage complicated their plans. Homes were hard to come by and returning veterans were forced to come up with creative living arrangements. They moved in with their parents or rented out basements, attics, garages, Quonset huts, carriage houses, even chicken coops. Levittown's rows of mass-produced houses, built by Abraham Levitt and his two sons, William and Alfred, alleviated the housing shortage, at least for the thousands of veterans approved to live there—a clause in the early leases excluded minority veterans. In William Levitt's own words: "We can solve a housing problem or we can try to solve a racial problem, but we cannot combine the two."

The first residents could only rent there—for $60 a month, with the option to purchase the house (for $7,500) once the lease expired after a year. That rule changed in 1949, when the builders decided to sell the houses for the increased price of $7,990 (requiring very little money down and a low monthly mortgage payment). "Levittown, Long Island, was the Model T of the American postwar generation," write Rosalyn Baxandall and Elizabeth Ewen in *Picture Windows.* For the returning soldier, it was a Kodachrome picture of the American dream—complete with a loving wife, new and improved appliances, a tidy lawn, and a young child pedaling a shiny tricycle down the sidewalk. Even the wholesome, ready-made street names (Schoolhouse Road, Barnyard and Buttercup Lanes, etc.) seemed to promise a safe, kid-friendly neighborhood.

The first three hundred families moved into the Island Trees community, as Levittown was initially called, on October 1, 1947. Just a few months later, residents started posting ads in the local newspapers. If we've forgotten that America's biggest baby boom occurred during this prosperous time, these black-and-white classifieds are colorful reminders (within the first decade, more than seven thousand children were baptized in the local Catholic church). Not far from the newspaper's "free babysitting listings" and "lost and found" notices (flush with child-related items—stray tricycles, lost Girl Scout pencils, the occasional baby blanket that blew into the neighbor's yard) is the swap section. Levittown was built on the principles of the assembly line, and suburban living fostered an appetite for consumer culture and brand names.

Residents of Levittown were expected to abide by a list of rules and regulations, set forth by the builders to "attain and maintain"

> **Will swap "Broil King" electric**
> broiler for lawn mower, or what
> have you. Hicksville 5-2250.
>
> —March 10, 1949,
> *Levittown Tribune*

> **SWAP**
> Will swap four tires, 6.50-16
> Firestone and General, for baby
> crib. HI 5-5073.
>
> —July 28, 1949,
> *Levittown Tribune*

> Will swap my Royal portable
> typewriter for a good electric
> sewing machine. Call Hicksville
> 5-4702-J.
>
> —September 2, 1948,
> *Levittown Tribune*

> Will swap Westinghouse hand
> vacuum, excellent condition,
> for good collapsible carriage. HI-5-
> 2438.
>
> —August 18, 1949,
> *Levittown Tribune*

the small-town feel of the suburban enclave. Among them, no fences: "You will see fences only in neighborhoods 'down at the heel', in 'shanty towns', and in 'goatville communities,'" declared Abraham Levitt. Lawns had to be cut and weeded weekly. Garbage could be stored only in a "closed metal receptacle" in the back of the house and "not more than one foot from it except when placed at the curb for collection." No clotheslines (too messy), but portable revolving dryers were allowed, in the backyard only, and "not on Saturdays, Sundays or holidays."

In his "Chats on Gardening" column in the *Levittown Tribune,* Abraham Levitt elaborated weekly on his philosophy for the town and its upkeep: "I would like to add to the slogan of 'A Garden Community' an addition: 'A Spotless Town.' For a place cannot be called attractive and beautiful unless at the same time it is neat, clean, tidy and spic and span." The swaps printed in the *Levittown Tribune* reflect the specific concerns of the community and the families who moved there.

swap

Online today, the boundaries of the neighborhood barter ex-change have dissolved. From digital listings, proposed swaps from a diverse and borderless community collective can be sorted through and analyzed: website design traded for Spanish lessons; acupunc-ture for the right couch; yard work for managed health care; two packs of cigarettes for almost anything. These postings, as earnest as any barter ads placed in the eighteenth century, continue to chronicle a quirky, often unpredictable angle of America's per-sonal history.

strange red cow

I'll teach you belly dance, you teach me Quickbooks

Reply to: anon@craigslist.org
Date: 2005-03-15, 11:12AM EST
Hi, I need to learn Quickbooks. I'm a professional dancer and I can give you belly dance classes in exchange. If you're interested, please email me. Women only - thanks.

—March 15, 2005, *www.craigslist.com* (New York, New York)

Glam Leopard-Print Scrubbing Brush for Spring Cleaning!

Reply to: anon@craigslist.org
Date: 2005-03-26, 7:24AM EST
Scrubbing brush with black bristles and leopard-print handle. Shows some minor use, but still cute!
Come by my office in midtown to pick it up.
In exchange I'll accept:
A few #10 envelopes
A can of green beans
A new 60-watt lightbulb
Some 37-cent stamps
A roll of toilet paper new in package
A roll of paper towels new in package
A roll of clear packing tape
A roll of invisible scotch tape
A can of soup, such as Campbell's Tomato, Campbell's Potato and Garlic, most Progresso soups
How about a book about investing, financial planning, writing, women's issues, life in Victorian or Edwardian times
...also open to suggestions.
Thanks!

—March 26, 2005, *www.craigslist.com* (New York, New York)

Epilogue

WANTED. Young, skinny, wiry fellows, not over eighteen. Must be expert riders, willing to risk death daily. Orphans preferred. Wages— $25 per week. Apply—Central Overland Pony Express Alta Building Montgomery Street.

—1860, newspaper title unknown

Legend has it that William W. Finney, an agent for the Central Overland California & Pike's Peak Express Company, better known as the Pony Express, inserted this notice in San Fransisco newspapers in 1860. This help-wanted posting is now one of America's most iconic classifieds, quoted in countless books and newspaper articles about that famous express mail service from Missouri to California. "It has become one of the most thrilling and romantic images associated with the legacy of the Pony Express," writes Christopher Corbett in *Orphans Preferred,* "and there is hardly a gift shop peddling Pony Express memorabilia from St. Joe to Old Sac that does not sell a quaint reproduction of this notice suitable for framing." Historians and Pony Express enthusiasts have scoured newspaper archives to find proof of an original; so far, no luck. Yet, in spite of any primary source evidence, the advertisement continues to stand as a symbol for that brave but short-lived postal enterprise.

Whether or not the notice ever ran in the newspaper is perhaps less intriguing than the fact that there is a desire to believe it did, that scores of writers have chosen to use it as a valid illustration of a moment in American history, and their readers, in turn, have come to trust those lines and the dramatic images that they evoke. This speaks to the cultural power of the classified advertisement: It is a concise, accessible format, easily recognizable to a great number of people. In just a few abbreviated lines, a classified can distill a scene, summarize a set of circumstances, and communicate a message—even, it seems, when the notice in question may or may not have officially appeared in print.

The ads collected in *Strange Red Cow* did appear in print—mostly in newspapers, some online, and a few in magazines and booklets of various sizes and scope. Still, each one must be reviewed with care and a discerning eye, as the reliability of a posting shifts with the intent of the advertiser. With nothing to sell and no marketing agenda to consider, an ad for a lost animal seems only to benefit from truth telling. Other classified categories are more complex: a "fresh breast of milk" offered by a poor wet nurse desperate for work may or may not have been as "fresh" as she publicly made claim, descriptions in runaway slave notices are suspect, and personal advertising was, and still is, rife with half-truths, even lies.

One of the clearest examples of the classified's capacity for bias is captured in those disparaging notices placed by husbands after their wives ran away. When a runaway wife responded, disputing those charges with a follow-up posting, she offered a different and conflicting perspective. Where the truth lies, we don't know. The classified advertisement does not tell the whole story; every word left out is another word the reader must try to fill in. But put into context, and compared to other ads over time, these notices reveal indisputable patterns in our society, and in their own, understated way, keep us accountable—to ourselves. Our habits, our practices, our principles are engraved in our classifieds, and touring those columns reunites us with our collective past.

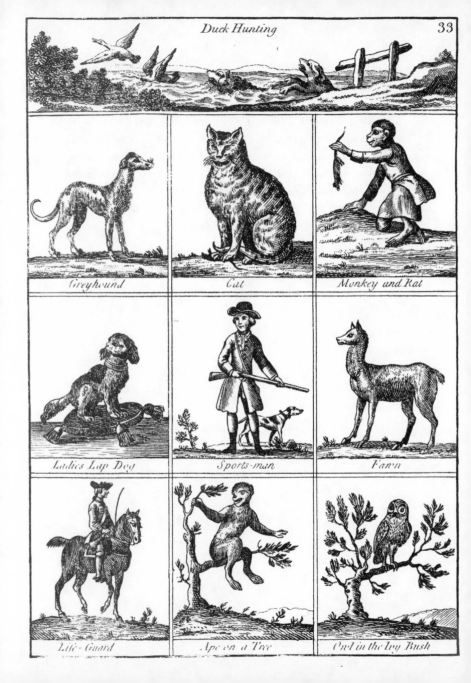

Greyhound

Cat

Monkey and Rat

Ladies Lap Dog

Sports-man

Fawn

Life-Guard

Ape on a Tree

Owl in the Ivy Bush

Notes

About This Book

xii: Newspaper classified advertising revenue statistics: "Newspaper Classified Advertising Expenditures," Newspaper Association of America, Feb. 2005, <www.naa.org>.

xiii: "Everybody's Column": *Rockland Courier-Gazette,* Aug. 12, 1899.

xiii: "People's Column": *Marion Daily Star,* Feb. 9, 1903.

Introduction

1: For background on advertising before the printing press see Frank Presbrey, *The History and Development of Advertising* (1929; New York: Greenwood Press, 1968), pp. 1–16; and Henry Sampson, *A History of Advertising from the Earliest Times* (London: Chatto and Windus, 1875), pp. 33–60.

1: "Siquis": Frank Presbrey, *History and Development of Advertising,* pp. 14–15.

1: "Smooth Black Dog, less then a Grey-hound": Presbrey, *History and Development of Advertising,* p. 50. Presbrey notes November 1660 as the date of this ad, but author found it in June 21–June 28, 1660 issue of *Mercurius Publicus.* The follow-up ad ran one week later.

1: "We must call upon you again for a Black Dog": *Mercurius Publicus,* June 28–July 5, 1660.

2: For history of the *Oxford Gazette* and the *London Gazette:* P. M. Handover, *A History of The London Gazette, 1665–1965* (London: Curwen Press, 1965), pp. 10–13.

2: Initially, advertisements were banned: Handover, *History of The London Gazette,* p. 16.

2: "The Countrey shall be furnished once a moneth": Presbrey, *History and Development of Advertising,* p. 119.

2: For background history of *Publick Occurrences Both Forreign and Domestick* see Charles E. Clark, *The Public Prints* (New York: Oxford University Press, 1994), pp. 71–73; also see Frank Luther Mott, *American Journalism: A History: 1690–1960* (New York: The Macmillan Company, 1962), pp. 9–10.

2: It was four pages long: Mott, *American Journalism,* p. 10.

2: "Without the least Privity or Countenance of Authority": Clark, *The Public Prints,* p. 73.

3: For background on newsgathering in the colonies before newspapers see Mott, *American Journalism,* pp. 7–8; also see Clark, *The Public Prints,* p. 73.

4: The advertisement for the lost anvils first appeared in the *Boston News-Letter,* April 24–May 1, 1704.

4: The advertisement for stolen clothing and America's premier real estate announcement appeared in the *Boston News-Letter,* May 1–8, 1704.

4: Circulation of the *Boston News-Letter* initially limited to 250 copies: Clark, *The Public Prints,* p. 78.

4: By 1765, eleven out of the thirteen colonies: Mott, *American Journalism,* p. 43.

4: For the origins of "classified" advertising departments: Mott, *American Journalism,* p. 506; in a price list of advertising rates printed in the *New York Times* on March 26, 1871, "ordinary classified advertisements" are listed at "20 cents per line each insertion."

1: Lost and Found

11: definition of *ozenbrigs* comes from Billy G. Smith and Richard Wojtowicz, *Blacks Who Stole Themselves: Advertisements for Runaways in the Pennsylvania Gazette, 1728–1790* (Philadelphia: University of Pennsylvania Press, 1989), p. 181; also see Thomas Costa, "Glossary of Terms," *The Geography of Slavery in Virginia Project,* University of Virginia's College at Wise, 2003, <www.vcdh.virginia.edu/gos/gloss.html>.

12: In 1736, the colony of New Jersey: James Green, Library Company of Philadelphia, e-mail to author, Dec. 17, 2003: also see Eric P. Newman, *The Early Paper Money of America* (Racine,

WI: Whitman Publishing Company, 1967), p. 180.

13: For background history of the diaper: Linda Baumgarten, *What Clothes Reveal: The Language of Clothing in Colonial and Federal America* (Williamsburg, VA: The Colonial Williamsburg Foundation/Yale University Press, 2002), p. 158.

13: Shoes to clocks to plows: Richard D. Brown, "Modernization: A Victorian Climax," in *Victorian America,* ed. Daniel Walker Howe (Philadelphia: University of Pennsylvania Press, 1976), p. 35.

15: "have some regular plan for employment of your time": Catharine Beecher, *Miss Beecher's Domestic Receipt Book,* 3rd ed. (New York: Harper & Brothers, 1850), p. 276.

15: "If one wanted to appear to be both busy and genteel": Beverly Gordon, "Victorian Fancywork in the American Home: Fantasy and Accommodation," Marilyn Ferris Motz and Pat Browne, eds., in *Making the American Home: Middle-Class Women & Domestic Material Culture, 1840–1940* (Bowling Green, OH: Bowling Green State University Popular Press, 1988), p. 51.

16: For symbolism of fancywork see Gordon, "Victorian Fancywork in the American Home," pp. 50–52.

16: Hair jewelry had long commemorated: C. Jeanenne Bell, *Collector's Encyclopedia of Hairwork Jewelry* (Paducah,

Kentucky: Collectors Books, 1998), pp. 8–12.

17: "The professional hair-manufacturers": C.S. Jones and Henry T. Williams, *Hair-Work & Other Ladies' Fancy Work* (1876; Berkeley, CA: Lacis Publications, 2003), p. 7.

17: Strands were braided, plaited, coiled: Ginny Redington Dawes and Corinne Davidov, *Victorian Jewelry: Unexplored Treasures* (New York: Abbeville Press, 1991), p. 140.

18: In 1888, when George Eastman: Naomi Rosenblum, *A World History of Photography*, rev. ed. (New York: Abbeville Press, 1984), p. 259.

20: "Fairs, holidays, fair-weather Sundays": Morton J.A. McDonald, *Getting and Keeping Classified Advertising* (New York: Prentice-Hall, 1936), p. 233.

23: As the cost of carriage production: Don H. Berkebile, ed., *American Carriages, Sleighs, Sulkies, and Carts* (New York: Dover Publications, 1977), pp. vi–vii.

29: Early records describe: William Cronon, *Changes in the Land: Indians, Colonists, and the Ecology of New England* (New York: Hill and Wang, 1983), pp. 22–24: also see David Freeman Hawke, *Everyday Life in Early America* (New York: Harper & Row, 1988), pp. 13–14.

29: Captain John Smith noted: Philip L. Barbour, ed., *The Complete Works of John Smith* (Chapel Hill: The University of North Carolina Press, 1986), 2: p. 225.

29: 128 cattle, 88 goats, and countless swine: Lyman Carrier, *The Beginnings of Agriculture in America* (New York: McGraw-Hill Book Company, 1923), p. 124.

29: "three heifers and a bull": quoted in Virginia DeJohn Anderson, "King Philip's Herds: Indians, Colonists, and the Problem of Livestock in Early New England," *William and Mary Quarterly*, 3rd ser., 51 (Oct. 1994), p. 602.

30: "Barbarism to Civilitie": quoted in Anderson, "King Philip's Herds," p. 605.

30: But for many Native Americans: ibid., pp. 605–608; also see Cronon, *Changes in the Land*, pp. 130–132.

32: Earmarks of various combinations: see Ruth Herndon, "'Breachy' Sheep and Mad Dogs: Troublesome Domestic Animals in Rhode Island, 1750–1800," in *New England's Creatures, 1400–1900: Annual Proceedings of the Dublin Seminar for New England Folklife*, Peter Benes, ed. (Boston, MA: Boston University Press, 1995), pp. 63–64; also Anderson, "King Philip's Herds," p. 615.

33: Fences also helped: see Ruth Herndon, "'Breachy' Sheep and Mad Dogs," pp. 64–65; also see Howard S. Russell, *A Long Deep Furrow: Three Centuries of Farming in New England* (Hanover: University Press of New England, 1982), pp. 18–20, 103–106.

34: "glittering shops," "lively whirl of carriages": Charles Dickens, *American Notes for General Circulation* (London: Chapman & Hall, 1850), pp. 55, 57.

36: Local city markets supplied meat: Edwin G. Burrows and Mike Wallace, *Gotham: A History of New York City to 1898* (New York: Oxford University Press, 1999), p. 477.

36: "Two portly sows": Charles Dickens, *American Notes for General Circulation*, p. 59.

36: "Every pig": ibid., p. 59.

36: ten thousand roaming pigs: John Duffy, *A History of Public Health in New York City, 1625–1866* (New York: Russell Sage Foundation, 1968), pp. 385–386.

37: over two hundred slaughterhouses: Duffy, *History of Public Health in New York City*, p. 381.

37: In 1853, the city's Common Council finally outlawed daytime cattle drives: Duffy, *History of Public Health in New York City*, p. 386.

37: "To recreate the atmosphere": Duffy, *History of Public Health in New York City*, p. 376.

38: an estimated 22,500 horses dragged public vehicles: Burrows and Wallace, *Gotham*, p. 787.

40: "I envisioned a line down the block": William Grimes, *My Fine Feathered Friend* (New York: North Point Press, 2002), p. 80.

40: "If anyone happens to see a fat black hen": William Grimes, *My Fine Feathered Friend*, p. 85.

41: "killing sheep and swine, biting horses and cattle:" quoted in Howard Chapin, *Dogs in Early New England*, (Providence, RI: Press of E. A. Johnson & Co., 1920) p. 6.

41: For changing relationship between humans and their pets in middle-class Victorian America, see Katherine C. Grier, "Animal House: Pet Keeping in Urban and Suburban Households in the Northeast, 1850–1900," in *New England's Creatures, 1400–1900: Annual Proceedings of the Dublin Seminar for New England Folklife*, Peter Benes, ed., pp. 109–129.

41: "Kindness towards animals is of great importance": Mrs. Child, *The Mother's Book*, 2nd ed. (1831; Old Sturbridge Village, MA: Applewood Books, 1992), pp. 6–7; for additional examples of similar childrearing advice and a discussion of the trend, see Katherine Grier, "Animal House," pp. 120–121.

42: "elegant in form and cheerful in disposition": *Book of Household Pets and How to Manage Them* (New York: Dick and Fitzgerald, Publishers, 1866), p. 81.

42: "Some exhibit excessive fondness": *Book of Household Pets*, p. 83.

42: "a very amusing companion": *Book of Household Pets*, p. 86.

44: first commercial pet stores in America: Grier, "Animal House," p. 114.

45: Major brand names: Maryann Mott, "Catering to the Consumers with Animal Appetites," *New York Times*, Nov. 14, 2004.

47: history of wampum: Richard Doty, *America's Money, America's Story* (Wisconsin: Krause Publications, 1998), pp. 7–9; also see Louis Jordan, "Wampum: Introduction," *The Coins of Colonial and Early America*, University of Notre Dame, Department of Special Collections, n.d., <www.coins.nd. edu/ColCoin/ColCoinIntros/ Wampum.intro.html>.

47: First mint in the colonies: Doty, *America's Money*, pp. 29–31.

47: Paper money appeared in 1690: Doty, *America's Money*, pp. 35–36, 39.

48: For a digital copy of *Father Abraham's Almanack*, see Louis Jordan, "Colonial Currency," University of Notre Dame, Department of Special Collections, n.d. <www.coins.nd.edu/ ColCoin/ColCoinImages/Tables>.

49: Continental currency: Doty, *America's Money*, pp. 48–49.

49: In 1792, the first United States coins were minted: ibid., pp. 73–76.

50: National Banking Act: ibid., p. 164.

50: National notes eventually replaced state bank bills: ibid., pp. 164–165.

50: Federal Reserve note: ibid., p. 196.

2: The Runaway Slave Notice

56: "Men and woman, old and young, married and single": Frederick Douglass, *Narrative of the Life of Frederick Douglass* (1845; Boston: The Anti-Slavery Office; New York: Dover Publications, 1995), p. 27.

56: In 1619, colonist John Rolfe: Ira Berlin, *Many Thousands Gone: The First Two Centuries of Slavery in North America* (Cambridge, MA: The Belknap Press of Harvard University Press, 1998), p. 29.

56: "A count of fugitive advertisements": Daniel Meaders, *Dead or Alive: Fugitive Slaves and White Indentured Servants Before 1830* (New York: Garland Publishing, 1993), p. 18.

56: For reasons why some slave owners did not advertise, see Daniel Meaders, "South Carolina Fugitives as Viewed Through Local Colonial Newspapers with Emphasis on Runaway Notices 1732–1801," *Journal of Negro History*, 60 (Apr. 1975), p. 291; see also John Hope Franklin and Loren Schweninger, *Runaway Slaves: Rebels on the Plantation* (New York: Oxford University Press, 1999), pp. 286–289.

57: For range and origin of slaves' names see Meaders, "South Carolina Fugitives as Viewed Through Local

Colonial Newspapers," pp. 311–312; Lorenzo J. Greene, "The New England Negro as Seen in Advertisements for Runaway Slaves," *Journal of Negro History*, 29, no. 2 (Apr. 1944), pp. 129–131; Ira Berlin, *Many Thousands Gone*, pp. 173–174; Judith Kelleher Schafer, "New Orleans Slavery in 1850 as Seen in Advertisements," *Journal of Southern History*, 47, no. 1 (Feb. 1981), pp. 52–53.

57: "Particularly prominent was the African practice": Berlin, *Many Thousands Gone*, p. 174.

58: More runaway notices for males than females: see Franklin and Schweninger, *Runaway Slaves*, pp. 210–213; Greene, "The New England Negro as Seen in Advertisements for Runaway Slaves," *Journal of Negro History*, 29, no. 2 (Apr. 1944), p. 132; Billy G. Smith and Richard Wojtowicz, *Blacks Who Stole Themselves: Advertisements for Runaways in the Pennsylvania Gazette, 1728–1790* (Philadelphia: University of Pennsylvania Press, 1989), p. 13; Meaders, *Dead or Alive*, pp. 33–35; Meaders, "South Carolina Fugitives as Viewed Through Local Colonial Newspapers," p. 292; Schafer, "New Orleans Slavery in 1850 as Seen in Advertisements," pp. 43–44; Lathan Algerna Windley, *A Profile of Runaway Slaves in Virginia and South Carolina from 1730 through 1787*

(New York: Garland Publishing, 1995), pp. 39–40.

60: References to height and size: see Windley, *A Profile of Runaway Slaves in Virginia and South Carolina*, p. 53.

61: Definition of fustian: Peter F. Copeland, ed., *Working Dress in Colonial and Revolutionary America* (Westport, CT: Greenwood Press, 1977), p. 202.

62: Heinous acts of physical abuse: see Franklin and Schweninger, *Runaway Slaves*, pp. 42–46.

62: Owners routinely shackled these iron devices: Meaders, "South Carolina Fugitives as Viewed Through Local Colonial Newspapers," p. 297; in *A Profile of Runaways Slaves in Virginia and South Carolina*, Lathan Windley includes a reference to an ad for "Jack and Nat, who got away ironed together" (*Virginia Gazette*, May 1, 1778), p. 117.

66: Runaways escaped in all seasons of the year: see Smith and Wojtowicz, *Blacks Who Stole Themselves*, pp. 11–12; also Greene, "The New England Negro," pp. 131–132.

67: Along with clothing, some runaways took objects: Lathan Windley, *A Profile of Runaway Slaves in Virginia and South Carolina*, pp. 114–116; Greene, "The New England Negro," pp. 140–141.

67: The difference in language between slave "For Sale" ads and notices for runaways: Meaders, "South Carolina Fugitives as Viewed Through Local Colonial Newspapers," pp. 288–289; Schafer, "New Orleans Slavery in 1850 as Seen in Advertisements," pp. 38–39.

69: Literate slaves could forge the documentation: Windley, *A Profile of Runaway Slaves in Virginia and South Carolina,* pp. 4–7; Franklin and Schweninger, *Runaway Slaves,* pp. 230–231; Graham Russell Hodges and Alan Edward Brown, eds., *"Pretends to be Free": Runaway Slave Advertisements from Colonial and Revolutionary New York and New Jersey* (New York: Garland Publishing, 1994), pp. xxvi–xxvii.

69: not all the information can be trusted: Meaders, *Dead or Alive,* pp. 28–32; Smith and Wojtowicz, *Blacks Who Stole Themselves,* p. 4.

69: A runaway known for his stuttering: Windley, *A Profile of Runaway Slaves in Virginia and South Carolina,* pp. 98–102.

69: "One must challenge, contest and raise questions": Meaders, *Dead or Alive,* p. 28.

69: "Ads were mug shots, not portraits": Kirsten Denise Sword, *Wayward Wives, Runaway Slaves and the Limits of Patriarchal Authority of Early America,* diss., Harvard University (Ann Arbor, MI: UMI Microform, 2002), p. 23.

71: In Virginia in 1705: cited by Windley, *A Profile of Runaway Slaves in Virginia and South Carolina,* pp. 25–26.

71: And the amount printed in the first advertisement: Franklin and Schweninger, *Runaway Slaves,* pp. 173–174.

71: The ad for "Neck" and "Benn" is cited in Franklin and Schweninger, *Runaway Slaves,* p. 173.

72: South Carolina passed a particularly cruel set of laws: Windley, *A Profile of Runaway Slaves in Virginia and South Carolina,* pp. 8–9.

73: "Upon the decease of my wife": quoted in Henry Wiencek, *An Imperfect God: George Washington, His Slaves, and the Creation of America* (New York: Farrar, Straus and Giroux, 2003), p. 4.

73: George Washington's advertisement is transcribed in full in Lathan A. Windley, "Runaway Slave Advertisements of George Washington and Thomas Jefferson," *Journal of Negro History,* 63, no. 4 (Oct. 1978), pp. 373–374.

73: "Three of them disappeared wearing Sunday clothes": Wiencek, *An Imperfect God,* pp. 99–100.

75: "Prison Fees in Maryld Neptune": Wiencek, *An Imperfect God,* p. 102.

75: "He knew slavery was evil": Willard Sterne Randall, *Thomas Jefferson: A Life* (New York: Henry Holt and Company, 1993), p. 144.

75: Thomas Jefferson's advertisement is transcribed in full in Windley, "Runaway Slave Advertisements of George Washington and Thomas Jefferson," p. 374.

77: He was caught: Randall, *Thomas Jefferson*, p. 144.

77: "The 1820 census reported that he held 44 slaves": Robert V. Remini, *Andrew Jackson and the Course of American Empire, 1767–1821* (New York: Harper & Row, 1977), p. 133.

77: Andrew Jackson's advertisement is transcribed in full in Robert P. Hay, " 'And Ten Dollars Extra, for Every Hundred Lashes Any person Will Give Him, to the Amount of Three Hundred': A Note on Andrew Jackson's Runaway Slave Ad of 1804 and on the Historian's Use of Evidence," *Tennessee Historical Quarterly*, vol. 36, no. 4 (Winter 1997), p. 468.

78: Advertisement for Andrew Johnson reproduced in Frank Presbrey, *The History and Development of Advertising* (New York: Greenwood Press, 1968), p. 185.

79: Crispus Attucks is considered: Robin D. G. Kelley and Earl Lewis, eds., *To Make Our World Anew: A History of African Americans* (New York: Oxford University Press, 2000), pp. 97–98.

80: sluggish and painstaking process of emancipation: Graham Russell Hodges and Alan Edward Brown, *"Pretends to be Free": Runaway Slave Advertisements from Colonial and Revolutionary New York and New Jersey* (New York: Garland Publishing, 1994), pp. xxxiv–xxxv; also see Ira Berlin, *Many Thousands Gone*, p. 234.

80: "Fugitive slave notices appeared in Monmouth County": Hodges and Brown, *"Pretends to be Free,"* p. xxxv.

80: Black codes after the Civil War replaced slave codes: Eric Foner, *Reconstruction: America's Unfinished Revolution, 1863–1877* (New York: Harper & Row, 1988), pp. 199–202.

81: "Indeed for many freedpeople the naming or renaming process": Ira Berlin, *Generations of Captivity: A History of African-American Slaves* (Cambridge, MA: The Belknap Press of Harvard University Press, 2003), pp. 260–261.

3: Information Wanted

87: Between 1845 and 1855, roughly one and a half million: Kirby A. Miller, *Emigrants and Exiles: Ireland and the Irish Exodus to North America* (New York: Oxford University Press, 1985) p. 291.

87: "In the pre-Famine decades emigrants sought 'independence'": Miller, *Emigrants and Exiles*, p. 298.

87: Disease swept through the ships: B. Emer O'Keeffe, ed., *The Search for Missing Friends: Irish Immigrant Advertisements Placed in the Boston Pilot*, vol. 6 (Boston: New England Historic Genealogical Society, 1997), p. i.

88: "Single persons were more mobile": Ruth-Ann M. Harris and Donald M. Jacobs, eds., *The Search for Missing Friends*, vol. 1 (Boston: New England Historic Genealogical Society, 1989), p. iv.

89: Beginning in 1831 and continuing on for the next eighty-five years: ibid., p. i.

89: "Irishman's Bible": O'Keeffe, ed., *The Search for Missing Friends*, vol. 8, p. iv.

89: "That all Irishmen should be interested in the circulation": *Boston Pilot*, letter to the editor, June 18, 1853.

91: Often spilling into several columns' worth of print space: In the January 1, 1853, issue of the *Boston Pilot*, for example, over 150 "Information Wanted" notices appeared.

91: For years, it cost an advertiser $1.00: B. Emer O'Keeffe, ed., *The Search for Missing Friends*, vol. 8, p. xviii.

91: "There is very little risk sending gold": *Boston Pilot*, January 16, 1869.

91: U.S. Census Bureau statistics: J.D.B DeBow, *Statistical View of the United States, Embracing its Territory, Population—White, Free Colored, and Slave—Moral and Social Condition, Industry, Property, and Revenue; The Detailed Statistics of Cities, Towns and Counties; Being a Compendium of the Seventh Census* (Washington: A.O.P. Nicholson, Public Printer, 1854), p. 399; also see Joseph C. G. Kennedy, *Population of the United States in 1860; Compiled from the Original Returns of the Eighth Census* (Washington, DC: Government Printing Office), p. 609.

92: "the hands which led Lake Erie downwards to the sea": O'Keeffe, ed., *The Search for Missing Friends*, vol. 8, p. xvi.

92: Construction work like the kind: ibid., p. xvi.

94: "Three-fourths of those advertised": ibid., p. xxvi.

94: "I have received satisfactory information": ibid., p. xxvi.

95: the government offered the massive reward: see Edwin M. Stanton, Secretary of War, *New York Times*, Apr. 21, 1865.

100: For a recounting of the kidnapping, the trail of ransom notes and the media whirlwind that followed, see Paula S. Fass, *Kidnapped: Child Abduction in America* (New York: Oxford University Press, 1997), pp. 21–22, 26–56; also see Christian K. Ross, *The Father's Story of Charley Ross, the Kidnapped Child: Containing a Full and Complete Account of the Abduction of Charles Brewster Ross* (Philadelphia: John E. Potter and Company, 1876), pp. 25–146.

101: he did not want to alarm his wife: "The reason for using officer Joyce's name instead of my own in the advertisement was to conceal the loss from Mrs. Ross; for I hoped that the child would be recovered before she would hear of his having been taken away," ibid., p. 39.

102: "You wil hav two pay us": quoted in Christian Ross, *The Father's Story*, p. 48.

102: "not compound the felony": Ross, *The Father's Story*, p. 88, as quoted in Fass, *Kidnapped*, p. 31.

102: "He can recite": Pinkerton's Detective Agency, *Abduction of Charlie Brewster Ross*, reward pamphlet (Philadelphia, August 22, 1874), p. 2.

102: "Wen you get ready to bisnes": Ross, *The Father's Story*, p. 70.

103: nothing more than a ploy: Norman Zierold, *Little Charley Ross: The Shocking Story of America's First Kidnapping for Ransom* (Boston: Little, Brown and Company, 1967), pp. 82–83.

105: "It's no use lying now": Ross, *A Father's Story*, p. 248.

105: invoked in future ransom notes and closing arguments: Paula Fass, *Kidnapped*, pp. 29, 54.

105: "Just after Walter Ross died in 1943": quoted in Paula Fass, *Kidnapped*, p. 26.

4: Personals

108: The English coined the personals the "agony column": Judy Harkison, " 'A chorus of groans,' notes Sherlock Holmes," *Smithsonian* (Sept. 1987), p. 196.

108: "I read nothing except the criminal news": Sir Arthur Conan Doyle, "The Adventure of the Noble Bachelor" in *The Illustrated Sherlock Holmes Treasury*, Revised & Expanded (New York: Avenel Books, 1984), p. 128.

108: "What a rag-bag of singular happenings!": Sir Arthur Conan Doyle, "The Red Tent" in *His Last Bow* (1917; Book-of-the-Month Club, Inc., n.p. 1994), p. 105.

111: "To the LADIES" personal ad: quoted in Irene Ktorides, "Marriage Customs in Colonial New England," *Historical Journal of Western Massachusetts*, 2, no. 2 (Fall 1973), p. 6.

111: "Every unmarried man in the township": ibid., p. 6.

112: "A woman ceased to exist if she married": Philip S. Foner, *Women and the American Labor Movement*, vol. 1 (New York: Free Press, 1979), pp. 10–11, quoted in Karen Shallcross Koziara, Michael H. Moskow, and Lucretia Dewey Tanner, eds., *Working Women: Past, Present, Future* (Washington, D.C.: The Bureau of National Affairs, Inc.), p. 3.

114: Records show that 10 percent of Union troops: Geoffrey C. Ward with Ric Burns and Ken Burns, *The Civil War: An Illustrated History* (New York: Alfred A. Knopf, 1990), p. 190.

118: "the full name and address of

every lady": *The Golden Seal Matrimonial Catalogue: Special Edition No. 250* (Tekonsha, MI: The Select Club, n.d.), p. 2, from the Thomas Parks Collection of Parks and McElrath Family Papers in the Southern Historical Collection, Manuscripts Department, Wilson Library, the University of North Carolina at Chapel Hill.

120: The directory . . . evolved into a social club for gay men: Daniel Harris, "Personals," *Antioch Review,* 55, no. 1 (Winter 1997), pp. 6–7.

121: the famous photographer Mathew Brady charged two dollars: Beaumont Newhall, *The Daguerreotype in America,* 3rd rev. ed. (New York: Dover Publications, 1975), p. 63.

121: The cost of a daguerreotype: Robert Taft, *Photography and the American Scene: A Social History, 1839–1889* (New York: Macmillan Company, 1938; New York: Dover Publications, 1964), pp. 78–84.

122: "make better pictures": Newhall, *The Daguerreotype in America,* p. 63.

122: History of carte de visite: Taft, *Photography and the American Scene,* pp. 138–141.

122: "You foolish girl that imagine yourself in love": *The Rogues and Rogueries of New-York: A Full and Complete Exposure of all the Swindles and Rascalities Carried On or Originated in the Metropolis* (New York: J. C. Haney & Co., 1865), p. 17.

125: "the one and only day": Janet Langlois, *Belle Gunness: The Lady Bluebeard* (Bloomington: Indiana University Press, 1985), pp. 5–6.

125: Philip's birth is shrouded in mystery. Some believe that Belle never gave birth to a child. See Langlois, *Belle Gunness,* pp. 56–57.

126: Advertisement placed by Belle Gunness is quoted in Lillian de la Torre, *The Truth About Belle Gunness* (New York: Fawcett Publications, 1955), p. 53; also see Sylvia Shepherd, *The Mistress of Murder Hill* (Bloomington, IN: 1st Books, 2001), p. 62.

126: "Chicago went crazy!": Langlois, *Belle Gunness,* p. 22.

127: the measurements were wrong: Shepherd, *The Mistress of Murder Hill,* pp. 25–26.

127: Lamphere offered conflicting confessions. In one version, he drove Belle to a railroad station on the night of the fire; in another, he drove her several miles away, where another man was waiting for her. See Shepherd, *The Mistress of Murder Hill,* pp. 221–224.

128: "a splendid desert": Mark Twain, *Daily Alta California* Aug. 11, 1867, as quoted in Phillip Lopate, ed., *Writing New York* (New York: Pocket Books, 1998) p. 257.

128: "You may sit in a New York restaurant": Mark Twain, *Daily Alta California,* June 30, 1867. Thanks to

Nellie Perera for bringing this article to my attention.

129: "There seems to be a pack of wooden-headed louts . . . catch these whelps!": Mark Twain, *Daily Alta California*, June 30, 1867.

5: Help Wanted

135: 37 million poured into American ports: Leonard Dinnerstein and David M. Reimers, *Ethnic Americans: A History of Immigration*, 4th ed. (New York: Columbia University Press, 1999), p. 17.

138: "It is general practice to prohibit mention": Morton J.A. McDonald, *Getting and Keeping Classified Advertising* (New York: Prentice-Hall, Inc., 1936), p. 255.

139: "There is scarcely a paper in America": ibid., p. 13.

140: Wage amounts, as well as the ages of the first workers, are cited in Brendan Francis Gilbane, "A Social History of Samuel Slater's Pawtucket, 1790–1830" (thesis, Boston University, 1969), pp. 123–124, 259.

141: By 1809, dozens of cotton mills were up and running: see Gary Kulik, Roger Parks, and Theodore Z. Penn, eds., Introduction, *The New England Mill Village, 1790–1860* (Cambridge, MA: The MIT Press, 1982), pp. 162–163.

141: meat, shoes, thread, ginger, tea, rum, etc.: For account records from the Slater-Tiffany mill, showing the range of items purchased at the company store, see Kulik, Parks, and Penn, eds., *The New England Mill Village*, pp. 415–425.

141: To deal with the chronic labor shortages: Paul E. Rivard, *A New Order of Things* (Hanover: University Press of New England, 2002), pp. 34–35, 97–98.

142: Definition of mule spinning: see Dr. Isabel B. Wingate, ed., *Fairchild's Dictionary of Textiles*, 6th ed. (New York: Fairchild Publications, 1996), p. 402.

143: In 1815, William Davis, his wife, and seven children: Kulik, Parks, and Penn, eds., *The New England Mill Village*, p. 416.

143: According to the company's account books: ibid., p. 421.

143: In 1827, the Slater-Tiffany mill downsized: ibid., p. 419.

143: payment was erratic: Caroline F. Ware, *The Early New England Cotton Manufacture: A Study in Industrial Beginnings* (1931; New York: Russell & Russell, 1966), pp. 245–247.

143: Once inside the factory: ibid., pp. 249–251.

144: The profile of the mill worker: Kulik, Parks, and Penn, eds., *The New England Mill Village*, p. xxix.

145: Newspaper advertising was generally *not* used: Caroline F. Ware, *The Early New England Cotton Manufacture*, pp. 213–214.

146: "sacred office": Sally McMillen, "Mothers' Sacred Duty: Breast-feeding Patterns among Middle- and Upper-Class Women in the Antebellum South," *Journal of Southern History*, 51, no. 3 (Aug. 1985), pp. 338–339.

146: worrisome complications: Janet Golden, *A Social History of Wet Nursing in America: From Breast to Bottle* (Columbus, OH: Ohio State University Press, 2001), p. 17.

147: Qualified candidates, their breasts full with milk: ibid., pp. 27–28.

148: "Careful inspection of the infant": ibid., p. 55.

149: if a woman needed work badly enough: ibid., p. 65.

150: "No More Wet Nurses!": Advertisement reproduced in Rima D. Apple, *Mothers & Medicine: A Social History of Infant Feeding, 1890–1950* (Madison, WI: University of Wisconsin Press, 1987), p. 9.

150: malt, cow's milk, sugar, and wheat flour: ibid., p. 9.

150: the Sears, Roebuck Company: ibid., pp. 140–142.

150: notice columns reflect this shift: Golden, *A Social History of Wet Nursing*, pp. 68–70.

151: a busy legal practice would have needed at least one copyist: Margery W. Davies, *Woman's Place Is at the Typewriter: Office Work and Office Workers, 1870–1930* (Philadelphia, PA: Temple University Press, 1982), p. 13.

151: "A neat handwriting is a letter of recommendation": James French, *Gentlemens' Writing Book* (Boston: James French, 1846) quoted in Tamara Plakins Thornton, *Handwriting in America: A Cultural History* (New Haven and London: Yale University Press, 1996), p. 43.

153: once a telltale sign of good character: ibid., p. 43.

6: Swap

155: definition of *swap*: *American Heritage Dictionary*, 3rd ed., s.v. "Swap."

155: "purchase" of Manhattan was supposedly a swap: Edwin G. Burrows and Mike Wallace, *Gotham: A History of New York City to 1898* (New York: Oxford University Press, 1999), pp. xiv–xv. Burrows and Wallace point out that while the Dutch understood the swap deal as a purchase of "a piece of property that could be owned and transferred," the Native Americans likely interpreted the transaction very differently.

156: Advertisement placed by Cowdery & Dutton transcribed in Annie Proulx, *What'll You Take for It?: Back to Barter* (Charlotte, VT: Garden Way Publishing, 1981), p. 12.

158: Boiled down in paper mills: Nicholson Baker, *Double Fold: Libraries and the Assault on Paper* (New York: Vintage Books, 2001), pp. 55–56.

159: Advertisement requesting "Fair Daughters of Liberty": Frank Luther Mott, *American Journalism: A History, 1690–1960* (New York: Macmillan Company, 1962), pp. 98–99.

159: 24 million pounds' worth in 1854 alone: Baker, *Double Fold*, p. 56.

159: two-fifths wood pulp and three-fifths rag: Mott, *American Journalism*, p. 402.

160: The first Depression-era "self-help" organization: Daniel J. Leab, "Barter and Self-Help Groups, 1932–33," *Midcontinent American Studies Journal*, 7, no. 1 (1966), pp. 15–24; also see Irving Bernstein, *The Lean Years: A History of the American Worker, 1920–1933* (Boston: Houghton Mifflin, 1972), pp. 416–420.

161: 159 barter groups in 127 cities of 29 American states: Malcolm Ross, "The Spread of Barter," *Nation*, 136 (March 1933), p. 228.

161: "a fresh sound egg, apple or potato": Jane Morgan Harris, R.N., "Bartering Potatoes and Eggs for Hospital Care," *Public Health Nursing*, 25, no. 7 (July 1933), p. 387.

161: "210 pounds of chicken, 100 bushels of potatoes": ibid., p. 387.

163: rented out basements, attics, garages: Rosalyn Baxandall and Elizabeth Ewen, *Picture Windows: How the Suburbs Happened* (New York: Basic Books, 2000), pp. 87–88; see also Lynne Matarrese, *The History of Levittown, New York* (Levittown Historical Society, 1997), p. 39.

163: "We can solve a housing problem": Lynne Matarrese, *The History of Levittown*, p. 44.

164: "Levittown, Long Island, was the Model T": Baxandall and Ewen, *Picture Windows*, p. 143.

164: more than seven thousand children were baptized: Matarrese, *The History of Levittown*, p. 50.

164: "attain and maintain": Abraham Levitt, "Chats on Gardening," *Levittown Tribune*, Nov. 22, 1951.

164: "You will see fences": Abraham Levitt, "Chats on Gardening," *Levittown Tribune*, Nov. 22, 1951.

165 "closed metal receptacle . . . curb for collection" . . . "not on Saturdays, Sundays or holidays": "Summary of Covenants and Restrictions of Levittown Ranch Homes" as reproduced in Lynne Matarrese, *The History of Levittown*.

165: "I would like to add to the slogan of 'A Garden Community' ": Abraham Levitt, "Chats on Gardening," *Levittown Tribune*, Nov. 22, 1951.

169: For history of the Pony Express ad see Christopher Corbett, *Orphans Preferred: The Twisted Truth and Lasting Legend of the Pony Express* (New York: Broadway Books, 2003), pp. 253–255.

169: "It has become one of the most thrilling": ibid., p. 253.

Selected Bibliography

Anbinder, Tyler. *Five Points: The 19th-Century New York City Neighborhood that Invented Tap Dance, Stole Elections, and Became the World's Most Notorious Slum.* New York: Plume, 2002.

Anderson, Virginia DeJohn. "King Philip's Herds: Indians, Colonists, and the Problem of Livestock in Early New England," *William and Mary Quarterly*, 3rd ser. 51, no. 4 (1994): pp. 601–624.

———. *Creatures of Empire: How Domestic Animals Transformed Early America.* New York: Oxford University Press, 2004.

Apple, Rima D. *Mothers & Medicine: A Social History of Infant Feeding, 1890–1950.* Madison: University of Wisconsin Press, 1987.

Baker, Nicholson. *Double Fold: Libraries and the Assault on Paper.* New York: Vintage Books, 2001.

Baumgarten, Linda. *What Clothes Reveal: The Language of Clothing in Colonial and Federal America.* Williamsburg, VA:The Colonial Williamsburg Foundation in association with Yale University Press, 2002.

Baxandall, Rosalyn and Elizabeth Ewen. *Picture Windows: How the Suburbs Happened.* New York: Basic Books, 2000.

Bell, C. Jeanenne. *Collector's Encyclopedia of Hairwork Jewelry: Identification and Values.* Paducah, Kentucky: Collector Books, 1998.

———. *Answers to Questions About Old Jewelry, 1840–1950.* Iola, WI: Krause Publications, 1999.

Berkebile, Don H., ed. *American Carriages, Sleighs, Sulkies, and Carts: 168 Illustrations from Victorian Sources.* New York: Dover Publications, 1977.

———. *Horse-Drawn Commercial Vehicles: 255 Illustrations of Nineteenth-Century Stagecoaches, Delivery Wagons, Fire Engines, etc.* New York: Dover Publications: 1989.

Berlin, Ira. *Many Thousands Gone: The First Two Centuries of Slavery in North America.* Cambridge, Mass.: The Belknap Press of Harvard University Press, 1998.

———. *Generations of Captivity: A History of African-American Slaves.* Cambridge, Mass.: The Belknap Press of Harvard University Press, 2003.

Bernstein, Irving. *The Lean Years: A History of the American Worker, 1920–1933.*

Boston: Houghton Mifflin Company, 1972.

Bernstein, Michael J. "Hair Jewelry, Locks of Love." *Smithsonian*, 6 no. 12 (1976): pp. 97–100.

Book of Household Pets and How to Manage Them. New York: Dick and Fitzgerald, Publishers, 1866.

Burrows, Edwin G., and Mike Wallace. *Gotham: A History of New York City to 1898.* New York: Oxford University Press, 1999.

Bushman, Richard L. *The Refinement of America: Persons, Houses, Cities.* New York: Vintage Books, 1992.

Campbell, Mark. *Self-Instructor in the Art of Hair Work, Dressing Hair, Making Curls, Switches, Braids, and Hair Jewelry of Every Description.* New York: M. Campbell, 1867.

Carlisle, Nancy C. "The Chewed Chair Leg and the Empty Collar: Mementos of Pet Ownership in New England" in *New England Creatures, 1400–1900: Annual Proceedings of the Dublin Seminar for New England Folklife.* Edited by Peter Benes. Boston: Boston University, 1995, pp. 130–146.

Carriage Collection, The. Stonybrook, NY: The Museums at Stony Brook Publishers, 1986.

Chapin, Howard M. *Dogs in Early New England.* Providence, RI: Press of E. A. Johnson & Co., 1920.

Child, L. Maria. *The Mother's Book.* Bedford, MA: Old Sturbridge Village/Applewood Books, 1992. First published by Carter and Hendee Publishers, 1831.

Clark, Charles E. *The Public Prints: The Newspaper in Anglo-American Culture, 1665–1740.* New York: Oxford University Press, 1994.

Clark, Charles E., and Charles Wetherell. "The Measure of Maturity: *The Pennsylvania Gazette, 1728–1765.*" *William and Mary Quarterly,* 3rd ser. 46, no. 2 (1989): pp. 279–303.

Coffin, Joseph. *Our American Money: A Collector's Story.* New York: Coward-McCann, Inc, 1940.

Cooper, Diana, and Norman Battershill. *Victorian Sentimental Jewellery.* South Brunswick: A. S. Barnes & Co., Inc., 1972.

Corbett, Christopher. *Orphans Preferred: The Twisted Truth and Lasting Legend of the Pony Express.* New York: Broadway Books, 2003.

Costa, Thomas. *The Geography of Slavery in Virginia: Virginia Runaways.* Wise, VA: University of Virginia's College at Wise, 2003. <http://people.uvawise.edu/runaways/>

Cressy, David. *Coming Over: Migration and Communication Between England and New England in the Seventeenth Century.* Cambridge: Cambridge University Press, 1987.

Cronin, William. *Changes in the Land: Indians, Colonists, and the Ecology of New England.* New York: Hill and Wang, 1983.

Crossen, Cynthia. "Classified Ads Tell Tales of Social Change: Sober Need Not Apply." *Wall Street Journal,* April 16, 2003.

Davies, Margery W. *Woman's Place Is at the Typewriter: Office Work and Office Workers, 1870–1930.* Philadelphia: Temple University Press, 1984.

Dawes, Ginny Redington, and Corinne Davidov. *Victorian Jewelry: Unexplored Treasures.* New York: Abbeville Press Publishers, 1991.

DeBow, J.D.B. U.S. *Statistical View of the United States, Embracing its Territory, Population—White, Free Colored, and Slave—More and Social Condition, Industry, Property, and Revenue; The Detailed Statistics of Cities, Towns and Counties; Being a Compendium of the Seventh Census.* Washington: A.O.P. Nicholson, Public Printer, 1854.

DeGrazia, Laura Murphy, and Diane Fitzpatrick Haberstroh, eds. *Irish Relatives and Friends: From "Information Wanted" Ads in the Irish-American, 1850–1871.* Baltimore: Genealogical Publishing Co., 2001.

De la Torre, Lillian. *The Truth About Belle Gunness.* New York: Fawcett, 1955.

Derr, Mark. *A Dog's History of America: How Our Best Friend Explored, Conquered, and Settled a Continent.* New York: North Point Press, 2004.

Diehl, Lorraine B. *Subways: The Track That Built New York City.* New York: Clarkson Potter/Publishers, 2004.

Dinnerstein, Leonard, and David M. Reimers. *Ethnic Americans: A History of Immigration,* 4th ed. New York: Columbia University Press, 1999.

Doty, Richard. *America's Money, America's Story: A Comprehensive Chronicle of American Numismatic History.* Iola, WI: Krause Publications, 1998.

Douglass, Frederick. *Narrative of the Life of Frederick Douglass.* New York: Dover Publications, 1955. First printed by Anti-Slavery Office, 1845.

Dunwell, Steve. *The Run of the Mill: A Pictorial Narrative of the Expansion, Dominion, Decline and Enduring Impact of the New England Textile Industry.* Boston: David R. Godine, Publisher, 1978.

Ellis, Joseph J. *His Excellency: George Washington.* New York: Alfred A. Knopf, 2004.

Ewing, F.W., ed. *The Hobby Directory: "Who's Who in Hobbies?"* no. 8 (June 1951).

Fass, Paula S. *Kidnapped: Child Abduction in America.* New York: Oxford University Press, 1997.

Fee, Elizabeth, and Steven H. Corey. *Garbage!: The History and Politics of Trash in New York City.* New York: New York Public Library, 1994.

Foner, Eric. *Reconstruction: America's Unfinished Revolution, 1863–1877.* New York: Harper & Row, 1988.

Frank, Robin Jaffee. *Love and Loss: American Portrait and Mourning Miniatures.* New Haven: Yale University Press, 2000.

Franklin, John Hope, and Loren Schweninger. *Runaway Slaves: Rebels on the Plantation.* New York; Oxford University Press, 1999.

Gilbane, Brandan Francis. "A Social History of Samuel Slater's Pawtucket, 1790–1830." Thesis, Boston University, 1969.

Golden, Janet. *A Social History of Wet Nursing in America: From Breast to Bottle.* Columbus: Ohio State University Press, 2001.

Green, Harvey. *The Light of the Home: An Intimate View of the Lives of Women in Victorian America.* New York: Pantheon Books, 1983.

Greene, Lorenzo J. "The New England Negro as Seen in Advertisements for Runaway Slaves." *Journal of Negro History,* 29, no. 2 (1944): pp. 125–146.

Grier, Katherine C. "Animal House: Pet Keeping in Urban and Suburban Households in the Northeast, 1850–1900" in *New England Creatures, 1400–1900,* Annual Proceedings of the Dublin Seminar for New England Folklife. Edited by Peter Benes. Boston: Boston University, 1995, pp. 109–129.

——. "Childhood Socialization and Companion Animals: United States, 1820–1870." *Society and Animals: Journal of Human-Animal Studies.* 7, no. 2 (1999), pp. 95–120.

Grimes, William. "It Came. It Clucked. It Conquered," *New York Times,* March 21, 2001.

——. "Lost: One Black Chicken. Owners Bereft," *New York Times,* April 4, 2001.

——. *My Fine Feathered Friend.* New York: North Point Press, 2002.

Handover, P. M. *A History of the London Gazette, 1665–1965.* London: The Curwen Press, 1965.

Harkison, Judy. " 'A Chorus of Groans,' notes Sherlock Holmes." *Smithsonian,* Sept. 1987, p. 196.

Harris, Daniel. "Personals," *The Antioch Review,* 55.1 (1997), pp. 6–24.

Harris, Jane Morgan, R.N. "Bartering Potatoes and Eggs for Hospital Care." *Public Health Nursing* 25 no. 7 (July 1933), pp. 386–387.

Harris, Ruth-Ann M., Donald M. Jacobs, and B. Emer O'Keeffe, eds. *The Search for Missing Friends: Irish Immigrant Advertisements Placed in the Boston Pilot.* 8 vols. Boston: New England Historic Genealogical Society, 1989–1999.

Hay, Robert P. " 'And Ten Dollars Extra, for Every Hundred Lashes Any Person Will Give Him, to the Amount of Three Hundred': A

Note on Andrew Jackson's Runaway Slave Ad of 1804 and on the Historian's Use of Evidence," *Tennessee Historical Quarterly*, 36, no. 4 (Winter 1977), pp. 468–478.

Hemphill, C. Dallett. *Bowing to Necessities: A History of Manners in America, 1620–1860*. New York: Oxford University Press, 1999.

Herndon, Ruth Wallis. "'Breachy' Sheep and Mad Dogs: Troublesome Domestic Animals in Rhode Island, 1750–1800." In *New England Creatures, 1400–1900*, Annual Proceedings of the Dublin Seminar for New England Folklife. Edited by Peter Benes. Boston: Boston University, 1995, pp. 61–72.

Higginbotham, Don, ed. *George Washington Reconsidered*. Charlottesville: University of Virginia Press, 2001.

Hindman, Hugh D. *Child Labor: An American History*. Armonk, NY: M. E. Sharpe, 2002.

Hodges, Graham Russell, and Alan Edward Brown, eds. *"Pretends to Be Free": Runaway Slave Advertisements from Colonial and Revolutionary New York and New Jersey*. New York: Garland Publishing, 1994.

Hook and the Book: The Emergence of Crochet and Knitting in American Popular Culture, 1840–1876. Nicole H. Scalessa, ed. Philadelphia: Library Company of Philadelphia, 2001. Exhibition catalog.

Hornung, Clarence. *Wheels Across America: A Pictorial Cavalcade Illustrating the Early Development of Vehicular Transportation*. New York: A. S. Barnes & Company, 1959.

Hornung, Clarence P., and Fridolf Johnson. *200 Years of American Graphic Art: A Retrospective Survey of the Printing Arts and Advertising Since the Colonial Period*. New York: George Braziller, 1976.

Howe, Daniel Walker, ed. *Victorian America*. Philadelphia: University of Pennsylvania Press, 1976.

Hunt-Hurst, Patricia. " 'Round Homespun Coat & Pantaloons of the Same': Slave Clothing as Reflected in Fugitive Slave Advertisements in Antebellum Georgia," *Georgia Historical Quarterly*, vol. 83, no. 4 (1999), pp. 727–740.

Jones, C. S., and Henry T. Williams. *Hair-Work and Other Ladies' Fancy Work*. Berkeley, CA: Lacis Publications, 2003. Reprint of *Ladies' Fancy Work, Hints and Helps to Home Taste and Recreation*. New York: Henry T. Williams, Publisher, 1876.

Kelley, Robin D.G. and Earl Lewis. *To Make Our World Anew: A History of African Americans*. New York: Oxford University Press, 2000.

Kennedy, Joseph C. G. *Population of the United States in 1860; Compiled from the Original Returns of the Eighth Census*. Washington, DC: Government Printing Office, 1864.

Kessler-Harris, Alice. *Out to Work: A History of Wage-Earning Women in the United States*, 20th Anniversary ed. New York: Oxford University Press, 2003.

Kessner, Thomas. *The Golden Door: Italian and Jewish Immigrant Mobility in New York City, 1880–1915*. New York: Oxford University Press, 1977.

Koziara, Karen Shallcross, Michael H. Moskow, and Lucretia Dewey Tanner, eds. *Working Women: Past, Present, Future*. Washington, DC: The Bureau of National Affairs, Inc., 1987.

Ktorides, Irene. "Marriage Customs in Colonial New England," *Historical Journal of Western Massachusetts* 2, no. 2 (1973), pp. 5–21.

Kulik, Gary, Roger Parks, and Theodore Z. Penn, eds. *The New England Mill Village, 1790–1860*. Cambridge, MA: The M.I.T. Press, 1982.

Langlois, Janet L. *Belle Gunness: The Lady Bluebeard*. Bloomington: Indiana University Press, 1985.

Lee, Alfred McClung. *The Daily Newspaper in America: The Evolution of a Social Instrument*. New York: The Macmillan Company, 1937.

"The Legend of Belle Gunness." LaPorte, IN: LaPorte County Historical Society, n.d., <www.alco.org/libraries/lcpl/belle.html>.

Leighton, George R. "Doing Business Without Money: Barter, Exchange, and Production in Dayton," *Harpers*, July 1933, pp. 156–169.

———. "They Call It Barter: The New Economics in Ohio and Iowa," *Harpers*, August 1933, pp. 314–324.

Leopold, Allison Kyle. *Cherished Objects: Living With and Collecting Victoriana*. New York: Clarkson Potter/Publishers, 1991.

———. "The Lost Art of Victorian Hair Work," Open Notebook, *Victorian Homes*. 7, no. 1 (1988), pp. 68–69, 86.

Lopate, Phillip, ed. *Writing New York: A Literary Anthology*. New York: Pocket Books, 1998.

Loving, Boyce. "The Barter System Extended to the Theatre in Virginia," *New York Times* Sept. 30, 1934.

Mason, Gregory. "Wives by Mail," *Scribner's Magazine*, 89, no. 5 (May 1931), pp. 533–536.

Matarrese, Lynne. *The History of Levittown, New York*. Levittown Historical Society, 1997.

McDonald, Morton J. A. *Getting and Keeping Classified Advertising*. New York: Prentice-Hall, Inc., 1936.

McGiffert, Michael, ed. *Trivia or a Collection of the Wit and Whimsy of Early America, in some cases not wholly unimportant (and veritable) of Advices, both Forreign & Domestick; offered by the Printer for the delectation of his Readers*. Williamsburg, VA: Institute of Early American History and Culture, 1978.

McMillen Sally. "Mothers' Sacred Duty: Breast-feeding Patterns Among Middle- and Upper-Class Women in the Antebellum South," *Journal of Southern History*, 51, no. 3, (August 1985), pp. 333–356.

Meaders, Daniel L. "South Carolina Fugitives as Viewed Through Local Colonial Newspapers with Emphasis on Runaway Notices 1732–1801," *Journal of Negro History* 60, no. 2 (April 1975), pp. 288–319.

———. *Dead or Alive: Fugitive Slaves and White Indentured Servants Before 1830.* New York: Garland Publishing, 1993.

———, ed. *Advertisements for Runaway Slaves in Virginia, 1801–1820.* New York: Garland Publishing, 1997.

Meier, Judith Ann Highley, comp. *Runaway Women: Elopements and Other Miscreant Deeds as Advertised in the Pennsylvania Gazette, 1728–1789.* Apollo, PA: Closson Press, 1993.

Michener, Ronald W. "Money in the American Colonies." *EH.Net Encyclopedia.* Robert Whaples, ed. June 9, 2003. <www.eh.net/encyclopedia/?article=michener.american.colonies.money>.

Miller, Kerby A. *Emigrants and Exiles.* New York: Oxford University Press, 1985.

Moran, William. *The Belles of New England: The Women of the Textile Mills and the Families Whose Wealth They Wove.* New York: St. Martin's Press, 2002.

Mott, Frank Luther. *American Journalism: A History: 1690–1960,* 3rd ed. New York: The Macmillan Company, 1962.

Mott, Maryann. "Catering to the Consumers with Animal Appetites." *New York Times* Nov. 14, 2004.

Motz, Marilyn Ferris, and Pat Browne, eds. *Making the American Home: Middle-Class Women & Domestic Material Culture, 1840–1940.* Bowling Green, OH: Bowling Green State University Popular Press, 1988.

Mullin, Gerald W. *Flight and Rebellion: Slave Resistance in Eighteenth-Century Virginia.* New York: Oxford University Press, 1972.

Murolo, Priscilla, and A. B. Chitty. *From the Folks Who Brought You the Weekend: A Short, Illustrated History of Labor in the United States.* New York: The New Press, 2001.

Newhall, Beaumont. *The Daguerreotype in America.* 3rd rev. ed. New York: Dover Publications, 1976.

Newman, Eric P. *The Early Paper Money of America.* Racine, WI: Whitman Publishing Company, 1967.

Parker, Freddie L., ed. *Stealing a Little Freedom: Advertisements for Slave Runaways in North Carolina, 1791–1840.* New York: Garland Publishing, 1994.

Presbrey, Frank: *The History and Development of Advertising.* New York: Greenwood Press, Publishers, 1968. First published 1929 by Doubleday & Company.

Proulx, Annie. *What'll You Take For It?: Back to Barter*. Charlotte, VT: Garden Way Publishing, 1981.

Purvis, Thomas L. *Colonial America to 1763*. New York: Facts on File, Inc., 1999.

Randall, Willard Sterne. *Thomas Jefferson: A Life*. New York: Henry Holt, 1993.

Remini, Robert V. *Andrew Jackson and the Course of American Empire, 1767–1821*, New York: Harper & Row, Publishers, 1977.

———. *The Life of Andrew Jackson*. New York: Penguin Books, 1990.

Rivard, Paul E. *A New Order of Things: How the Textile Industry Transformed New England*. Hanover, NH: University Press of New England, 2002.

Robbins, L. H. "Jobless Thousands Organize to Barter Labor and Goods," *New York Times*, January 22, 1933.

Robbins, Trina. *Tender Murderers: Women Who Kill*. York Beach, ME: Conari Press, 2003.

Rogues and Rogueries of New-York, The: A Full and Complete Exposure of all the Swindles and Rascalities Carried on or Originated in the Metropolis. New York: J. C. Haney & Co., Publishers, 1865.

Ross, Christian K. *The Father's Story of Charley Ross, the Kidnapped Child: Containing a Full and Complete Account of the Abduction of Charles Brewster Ross*. Philadelphia: John E. Potter and Company, 1876.

Ross, Malcolm. "The Spread of Barter," *Nation*, 136 (March 1933), pp. 228–229.

Rowell, Geo. P., comp. *Centennial Newspaper Exhibition*. New York: Geo. P. Rowell & Co., 1876.

Russell, Howard S. *A Long, Deep Furrow: Three Centuries of Farming in New England*. Hanover: University Press of New England, 1982.

Sampson, Henry. *A History of Advertising from the Earliest Times: Illustrated by Anecdotes, Curious Specimens, and Biographical Notes*. London: Chatto and Windus, 1875.

Scee, Trudy Irene. "A Bird for a Bonnet: Gender, Class, and Culture in American Birdkeeping, 1750–1990." Ph.D. diss., University of Maine, 1994.

Schaefer, Laura J. "Looking for Love, Online or on Paper," Op-ed, *New York Times*, Feb. 14, 2003, late ed.

Schafer, Judith Kelleher. "New Orleans Slavery in 1850 as Seen in Advertisements." *Journal of Southern History* 47 no. 1 (February 1981), pp. 33–56.

Schlereth, Thomas J. *Victorian America: Transformations in Everyday Life, 1876–1915*. New York: Harper Perennial, 1991.

Shepherd, Sylvia. *Mistress of Murder Hill.* Bloomington, Indiana: 1st Books Library, 2001.

Sherwood, David. "Take My Wife— prithee," *American Heritage* (April/May 1984).

Sigourney, Mrs. L. H. *Letters to Mothers.* Hartford: Hudson and Skinner, Printers, 1838.

Sloan, Eric. *A Museum of Early American Tools.* New York: Dover Publications, 2002. First published 1964 by Funk & Wagnalls.

Smith, Billy G., and Richard Wojtowicz, eds. *Blacks Who Stole Themselves: Advertisements for Runaways in the Pennsylvania Gazette, 1728–1790.* Philadelphia: University of Pennsylvania Press, 1989.

Speight, Alexanna. *The Lock of Hair.* Berkeley, California: Lacis Publications, 2004. Reprint of *The Lock of Hair: Its History, Ancient and Modern, Natural and Artistic: With the Art of Working in Hair,* 1872.

Stampp, Kenneth M. *The Peculiar Institution: Slavery in the Ante-Bellum South.* New York: Alfred A. Knopf, 1956.

Sutphen, Dick. *The Mad Old Ads.* New York: McGraw-Hill Book Co., 1966.

Sword, Kirsten Denise. *Wayward Wives, Runaway Slaves and the Limits of Patriarchal Authority in Early America.* Ph.D. diss., Harvard University, 2002.

Taft, Robert. *Photography and the American Scene.* New York: Dover Publications, 1964. First published 1938 by Macmillan Company.

Taylor, Alan. *American Colonies.* New York: Viking, 2001.

Thomas, Isaiah. *The History of Printing in America.* New York: Weathervane Books, 1970.

Thornton, Tamara Plakins. *Handwriting in America: A Cultural History.* New Haven, CT: Yale University Press, 1996.

Thurston, Mary Elizabeth. *The Lost History of the Canine Race: Our 15,000-Year Love Affair with Dogs.* Kansas City, MS: Andrews and McMeel, 1996.

Ward, Geoffrey C., Ric Burns, and Ken Burns. *The Civil War: An Illustrated History.* New York: Alfred A. Knopf, 1990.

Ware, Caroline. *The Early New England Cotton Manufacture: A Study in Industrial Beginnings.* New York: Russell & Russell, 1966.

Wiencek, Henry. *An Imperfect God: George Washington, His Slaves and the Creation of America.* New York: Farrar, Straus and Giroux, 2003.

Wilson, Charles Morrow. *Let's Try Barter,* 2nd rev. ed. Old Greenwich, CT: The Devin-Adair Co., 1976.

Windley, Lathan A. "Runaway Slave Advertisements of George Washington and Thomas Jefferson," *Journal of Negro History*, 63, no. 4 (1978), pp. 373–374.

———. *A Profile of Runaway Slaves in Virginia and South Carolina from 1730 Through 1787.* New York: Garland Publishing, 1995.

Zierold, Norman. *Little Charley Ross: The Shocking Story of America's First Kidnapping for Ransom.* Boston: Little, Brown and Company, 1967.

Zinn, Howard. *A People's History of the United States, 1492–Present.* New York: HarperCollins Publishers, 1980.

Acknowledgments

This book would still be an idea in waiting were it not for a number of people who helped me turn it into print. My first thanks goes to Andrew Carroll, who, when I contacted him out of the blue several years ago, encouraged me to write a proposal, then helped me shape it so it would sell. Amy Thesing, graphic artist extraordinaire, brought that first round of classifieds to life. Christina Clifford offered excellent advice when I needed it early on, and Laura Palmer generously led me to an agent. Many thanks to Amy Williams, at Collins McCormick, for her enthusiasm from the start and guidance throughout. I am also indebted to Chris Pavone at Clarkson Potter for taking an interest in the project and setting it on course, and to Jen DeFilippi, who with humor and a clear sense of direction, kept me and thousands of unruly advertisements on track. I am grateful, too, to Jenny Beal and Marysarah Quinn for creating the book's sharp and satisfying design, and to Mark McCauslin and Linnea Knollmueller for shepherding the book through production.

Though the majority of the advertisements included in this collection were found by examining newsprint and microfilm, page by page, my research benefited greatly from a handful of bound collections published over the years. *The Search for Missing Friends,* an eight-volume series covering the long run of Irish-American "information wanted" advertisements printed in the *Boston Pilot,* was an invaluable resource. In building the runaway-slave notice chapter I relied on the research and context provided by, among others, Alan Edward Brown, John Hope Franklin, Graham Russell Hodges, Daniel Meaders, Freddie L. Parker, Loren Schweninger, Billy G.

Smith, Lathan A. Windley, and Richard Wojtowicz. Digitally, Professor Thomas Costa's database of runaway slave ads, accessible through the Virginia Center for Digital History, put eighteenth-century Virginia postings at my fingertips. Accessible Archives made searching the *Pennsylvania Gazette* and nineteenth-century African-American newspapers a matter of keystrokes.

Many individuals and archives made the process of researching, writing, and reproducing these classifieds less daunting. Charlene Peacock, Erika Piola, Cornelia King, and James Green offered friendly assistance and access to the excellent holdings of the Library Company of Philadelphia; Patricia Boulos helped me reproduce classifieds from the Boston Athenaeum's extensive newspaper archive; Jaclyn Donovan and Philip Lampi made it possible to include ads from the extraordinary historic newspaper collection at the American Antiquarian Society; Leon Jackson shared his nineteenth-century swap ads with me, and imparted some helpful tips about writing and sticking with it; Robert Hoge of the American Numismatic Society patiently fielded my many money inquiries; Sylvia Shepherd helped me sort through the conflicting accounts of the Belle Gunness story; I am especially indebted to Virginia DeJohn Anderson of the University of Colorado, Stephanie Coontz of Evergreen State College, Janet Golden of Rutgers University, Graham Russell Hodges of Colgate University, and Gary Kulik of the Winterthur Museum, all of whom generously read over excerpts of the book, and offered helpful feedback.

Thanks, too, to Meredith Paine Sorozan at the Rhode Island Historical Society; Louis Jordan at the Department of Special Collections, University of Notre Dame Libraries; Ronald Michener at the University of Virginia; Larry Bacon at the Kennebec Historical Society; Roy Wells at the Maine State Library; Carol Jones at the Charleston Library Society; Andrian Paquette at the Slater Mill

Historic Site; Joshua Ruff at the Long Island Museum; Craig New-mark and Jim Buckmaster at Craig's List; Campbell Gibson at the U.S. Census Bureau; Polly Dwyer at the Levittown Historical Society; Sarah McNair Vosmeier at Hanover College; Gary Chilcote at the Patee House Museum; Christopher Corbett of the University of Maryland–Baltimore County; Christie Romero at the Center for Jewelry Studies; Carol Elkins at Sotheby's; James Damron at the United States National Slavery Museum; Kaitlin Shinnick at Skinner Auctioneers; Kristin Aguilera at the Museum of American Financial History; Susie Richter at the LaPorte County Historical Society Museum; Paul Needham at Princeton University's Scheide Library; Park Ranger Bill Warder, Colonial National Park; Mary Thompson of Mount Vernon Ladies' Association; Mary Mallia and Doris Hendershot at the Textile Museum; Nicholas Smith of the Rare Books Department, University Library, Cambridge; Jim Pettengell and Kenneth Schwarz at Colonial Williamsburg; Steve DeVillez and Eric Jackson at the National Underground Railroad Museum; Cathy Jonathan at the Gemological Institute of America; David Wooters and Kathy Connor at the George Eastman House; my gratitude also goes out to Don Plummer; Joyce Jonas; Ruth Gordon; Larry Carpenter; Leila Cohoon; Joe Nardone; Yuwie Tantipech; and David Eicher, Civil War historian and managing editor of *Astronomy* magazine.

Friends far and near cheered me on along the way. Josie Peltz, Leah Williams, Allison Saltzman, and Michael Deas offered valuable words of advice. Emilia Pisani gave me the encouragement and gentle push that I needed to move from the research phase—which could have gone on forever—to the writing. I am grateful to Christina George for carving the perfect cover woodcut, finding some of the classifieds included in the book, and lending a skilled hand whenever I needed it. My good friends, Nellie Perera and

Elizabeth Redwine, always improved my writing and my state of mind.

I could not have written this book without the love and constant support from my family. My parents, Beverly and Lawrence Bader, the best researchers I know (if it exists out there, they will find it) taught me early on to never stop looking for what matters. My sister, Rachel Bader, and brother-in-law, Leon Lazaroff, sharpened my words and rooted for me every step of the way. I am also grateful to the Duvall family, and to the late Jean Duvall for her ever-positive outlook.

Several years ago, this project moved into our home, and I am grateful to both John and Will Duvall for making so much room for it. I thank Will for teaching me many things, including what the "strange red cow" must have looked like. And to John, I dedicate this book. His wise and generous ways have made me a better writer and a better person.

Credits

The author gratefully acknowledges the following institutions and individuals for permission to reproduce original advertisements throughout the book.

American Antiquarian Society for the ads from the *Boston News-Letter* (pp. 3, 28), the *Georgia Gazette* (pp. 31, 33), the *New York Herald* (pp. 53, 95, 131), the *Massachusetts Spy or, American Oracle of Liberty* (pp. 49, 159), the *Boston Gazette, or Weekly Journal* (p. 79), the *Daily Memphis Avalanche* (p. 81), the *Providence Gazette* (p. 140), the *Pawtucket Chronicle and Rhode-Island and Massachusetts Register* (p. 144), and the *Portsmouth Journal of Literature and Politics* (p. 145).

Brent Andersen for the ad from the *Washington City Paper* (p. 133).

Anton Community Newspapers for the *Levittown Tribune* ads (pp. 165–166).

Boston Athenaeum for the ads from the *Boston News-Letter* (p. 7), the *Richmond Daily Dispatch* (pp. 18, 20, 35), the *Boston Evening Transcript* (pp. 19, 152), the *Rhode-Island American, and General Advertiser* (pp. 26, 96), the *Boston Pilot* (pp. 85, 94), the *Exeter News-Letter and Rockingham County Advertiser* (p. 96), and the *Boston Evening-Post* (p. 111).

Kimberly Brittingham for the "Glam Leopard-Print Scrubbing Brush" ad, www.craigslist.com (p. 167).

The Library of Congress for the ads from the *Tennessee Gazette* (p. 76) and the *Philadelphia Public Ledger* (pp. 100, 101, 103).

Maryland State Archives for George Washington's runaway-slave ad in the *Maryland Gazette* (p. 74), Special Collections (Maryland State Law Library Collection of the Maryland Gazette), August 20, 1761, MSA SC 2311-1-9.

Sucheta Sharma for the ad from the *Stranger* (p. 133).

Swaab Publishing for the ad from www.isawyou.com (p. 133). © Swaab Publishing.

Village Voice Media, Inc. for the ads on p. 119–120. © 1971, 1974, 2002 Village Voice Media, Inc. Reprinted with permission of the *Village Voice*.

Yankee Publishing, Inc. for *Yankee* ads (pp. 138, 162, 163). Reprinted with permission of Yankee Publishing, Inc., as seen in *Yankee* magazine (December, 1935; November, 1936; June, 1937; July, 1937; August, 1937; November, 1937; October, 1938; February, 1940; July 31, 2004).

Goody Gruntums Farm

Dame Partlet's Farm

Roger Swillum's House

Index

About the Author

SARA BADER is a freelance researcher and associate producer who has worked on historical documentary films for both A&E and The History Channel. Previously, she worked on the public affairs series *Frontline* and MSNBC's *Edgewise* with John Hockenberry. This is her first book.

UCTION.
BROWNE & NICHOLS WILL SELL, THIS DAY,
THURSDAY, MAY 16,

At 1 o'clock, in front of salesroom, 35 Nassau street,
ery fine pair long tailed black Horses, 15¼ hands high, 7
8 years old, perfectly sound, kind and gentle in any har-
s and first rate saddle horses; they have been in the coun-
all winter; are sold only for want of use; they are a beau-
l pair and worthy the attention of any gentleman in want
a first rate pair of horses.
ALSO,
rge assortment of Top and no Top Wagons,
One second hand jump seat Wagon,
One second hand Phaeton,
ogether with double and single Harness.
New and second hand.

UCTION NOTICE.—A LARGE AND DESIRABLE AS-
sortment of every description of Household Goods will
old at panic prices, at private sale, for two days, at 15
ton place, a few doors west of Broadway. New and
nd hand Carpets; large and small Pier and Mantel Mir-
s; rosewood Parlor and Chamber Suits, of every possible
ety; fine Hair Mattresses, Beds and Bedding, Lounges,
y Chairs, gilt and plain enamelled Chamber Suits; one su-
or rosewood seven octave Piano; Lace and Brocatel Win-
Drapery; Mantel clocks and Ornaments; Table Ware
Kitchen Utensils. Will be sold at one half their value.
above assortment embraces everything necessary for
teel housekeeping. Please call and examine before going
uction or purchasing elsewhere.

UCTION NOTICE.—M. DOUGHTY, AUCTIONEER,
will sell this day (Thursday), May 16, commencing at
o'clock, at salesrooms 85 Nassau street, handsome House-
Furniture, consisting of three rosewood framed Parlor
s, covered in crimson and maroon brogatel; black walnut
covered in green plush; mahogany do, covered in hair
, consisting of Tete-a-Tetes, Parlor, Arm and Reception
rs, two rich gilt frame Pier Glasses, Brussels and Ingrain
pets; a fine line of Oil Paintings in rich gilt frames; rose-
and mahogany Secretary and Library Bookcases, marble
Centre and side Tables, rosewood Etegere, mirror doors
back; rosewood 6½ octave Pianoforte; black walnut
ets, oak, mahogany and black walnut Extension Dining
es, Dining Chairs mahogany, black walnut and rosewood
ble top Dressing Bureaus, Bedsteads and Washstands to
ch; Hair Mattresses, Lounges, Wardrobes, &c, the whole
e peremptorily sold.

ACTION NOTICE.—A SOLID ROSEWOOD PARLOR
Suit, covered in the very best of French satin brocatel;
$250, will be sold for $125; one do in crimson reps for
als°, one double black walnut Parlor Suit, covered in
n plush, will be sold for $115; a lot of parlor, bed and
ng room Furniture. Apply this day at 72 Sixth avenue,
door below Waverley place. E. ROTH.

UCTION NOTICE.—A FAMILY DECLINING HOUSE.
keeping, will dispose of at private, all their Parlor,
mber and Dining room Furniture, at a great sacrifice, viz;
ed rosewood, seven octave Pianoforte, fully warranted;
$500, for $250, including stool and cover; Parlor Suits
$300, for $140, for $100 Carpeting, Bedding, Oil Paintings,
The furniture was all made to order for the present
er, been in use but five months, in excellent order. In-
e at No. 70 West Twenty-sixth street, near Sixth avenue.

JCTION NOTICE.—B. A. CHILTON, AUCTIONEER.
COLE & CHILTON will sell at auction, on Thursday,
16, at one o'clock, in front of their office, No. 45 Nassau
t, a sorrel Mare, eight years old, and fifteen hands high,
ectly sound and fast (can go in three minutes to the pole),
is a very easy trotter under the saddle; would make a
military horse, as she has great endurance and is always
the bit; sold only for want of use. Sale positive; terms
She cost the present owner $450.

JCTION NOTICE.
Large sale of new and second hand Vehicles, such as
aways, Phaetons, top Buggies, Road Wagons, &c., &c;
ingle and double Harness, by EZRA LUDLOW, Jr., at
ew salesrooms, 85 Liberty street, one door west of Broad-
this day, at 12 o'clock. Sale peremptory, to close con
ments.

richly carved seven octave Pianoforte, large Pier and Mantel
Mirrors, ormolu Chandeliers, Clocks and Mantel Ornaments;
large Vases, fine Paintings and Engravings, Marble Statuary,
&c,; rosewood Centre Table, statuary top. Japanese Fancy
Table, marble top, Velvet Carpets, &c Dining Room—Rosewood Extension Table, Chairs, covered in rep; oak Cornices
and Draperies Buffet, gold band Dinner Set, Tea do, fine
silver plated Ware, Glass, &c. Library—Solid oiled walnut
Bookcase and Chairs. Bedrooms—Brussels Carpets, rosewood carved Bedsteads, Bureaus, Amour a Glace, Wardrobes,
Chairs, &c; mahogany do, Cottage Suit, Mattresses and
Beds, Cabinets, Oilcloths, Sewing Machine, Hobby Horse,
&c, and other fine Furniture The sale will commence with
front basement, the kitchen ware having been disposed of.
Also at one o'clock, in front of the door, a superior and well
matched team of Pony Horses, eight years old, sound, kind
and gentle; both fine saddle horses; have trotted together,
carrying 500 pounds, 5 miles in 18 minutes. Also light top
Wagon, with pole and shafts, Blankets. Sheets, Robes, &c,
the whole forming a very fine establishment. Sale without
reserve.

HENRY H. LEEDS & CO. AUCTIONEERS.—HENRY
H. LEEDS & CO. will sell at auction, on Friday, May
17, at 10½ o'clock, at 112 Leonard street. Household Furni-
ture—consisting of Brussels and Ingrain Carpets; mahoga-
ny Sofas and Chairs, in hair cloth; mahogany marble top
Centre Tables; gilt frame French plate Pier Mahogany Sec-
retary, Bookcase; Clicloths; mahogany and black walnut
Bedsteads: do. Washstands; mahogany marble top Dressing
Bureaus; Hair Mattresses; Straw Mattresses, Bolsters and
Pillows, Crockery, Glass and Kitchen Ware.

HENRY H. LEEDS, AUCTIONEER.—HENRY H.
LEEDS & CO. will sell at auction, on Friday, May 17,
at 11 o'clock, in the gallery over the salesroom No 23 Nassau
street, fine collection of modern Oil Paintings, being the entire Gallery of a gentleman leaving for Europe, consisting of
the works of Williams, Boddington, Shayer, Jr., Combould,
Cooper, Quidor, Criswick Taylor, Armfield and others of
equal celebrity; also the "Sybil" by Huntington and many
valuable and rare works, all of which will be sold without
reserve. They will be ready for exhibition on Wednesday,
as above, with catalogues.

HANDSOME HOUSEHOLD FURNITURE
AT PUBLIC AUCTION.
$12,000 worth of
ELEGANT FIRST CLASS FURNITURE,
The property of a family removing to the country.
This day (Thursday), commencing at 11 o'clock, the beautiful
Parlor, Dining room, Chamber and Library Furniture in the
dwelling house, No. 152 Twenty-first street, between Seventh
and Eighth avenues, all of which is new, having been recently
made, and comprises everything adapted to a fashionable and
elegantly furnished residence—the whole to be peremptorily
sold for cash, consisting of English Velvet and Tapestry Carpets, elegant rosewood Parlor Furniture, en suite, comprising
three full suits, richly carved, all of which are covered in rich
silk brocatel, and of the best description Rosewood Centre and
Pier Tables; Turkish Chairs, in blue and gold satin and moquet;
Velvet Turkish Lounges, rich Mantel and Pier Mirrors, da-
mask and lace Curtains, gold and landscape Shades, two rosewood Etegeres, style of Louis XIV.; rich Sevres and Dresden
Mantel Vases; Bisque Figures; Artistic Bronzes, Parlor Ornaments, &c.
ELEGANT 7 OCTAVE PIANOFORTE.
MUSIC CABINET, STOOL AND COVER.
Marble top Bureaus, rich carved Bedsteads, twenty large
Hair Mattresses, Tete-a-Tetes, Chamber Suits in rosewood
bronze Clocks, marble Washstands, Lounges, French and
Spring seat Chairs, Rockers, Divans, Ottomans, Oval Mirrors,
superb Beds and Bedding, oak Extension Table, two fine mahogany Sofa Bedsteads, rich French and Bohemian China,
rich Tea Sets, Silver Ware, Spoons, Forks, Casters, Ice Pitch-
ers, Urns, Tea Service, ruby and chrystal Cut Glass of every
description; oak marble top Buffet, oak Chairs, superb oak
Desk, Oilcloth, rich Chandeliers, marble Hall Stand, one of
Wilder's Iron Safes Catalogues at house. Sale positive, rain
or shine. Sale commences at 2 o'clock precisely in the dining
room, the Kitchen Furniture having been disposed of
R. W. WESTCOTT, Auctioneer.

HENRY B. HERTS, JR., AUCTIONEER.
Peremptory sale of
Jeweller's Tools,
Splendid Chronometer Regulator, with illuminated dial;

BOARD... AND THEIR WIVES, OR single gentlemen, can obtain good Rooms, with Board, in the house lately fitted up. No. 36 Beach street, opposite St. John's park. Gas and bath in the house

BOARD.—ROOMS TO LET, WITH BOARD, ON THE second and third floors, front, suitable for gentlemen and their wives or single gentlemen. Location unsurpassed. Apply at 118 West Twenty-third street References required.

BOARD.—TO LET, WITH BOARD, AT NO. 137 SECOND avenue, between Eighth and Ninth streets, one nicely furnished front Room, on second floor, and one on third floor, with secretary bedstead in each, on moderate terms for the summer. References exchanged.

BOARD.—A PLEASANT SUIT OF ROOMS TO LET ON second and third floors, separate or together, to gentlemen and their wives or single gentlemen. Dinner at 2 o'clock. Pleasant and desirable location. References exchanged Call for three days at 268 West Twenty-second street.

BOARD FOR ONE OR TWO GENTLEMEN, AT BEDford, Brooklyn, with a private English family. No other boarders Large garden, good stabling, pleasantly located in the country, with two lines of cars every five minutes. Address B, box 120 Herald office.

BOARD AT 25 STUYVESANT STREET (CONTINUAtion of Astor place).—A gentleman and wife or two single gentlemen can be accommodated with Board, where the comforts of a home and choice of rooms secured, at the new English basement house east of Third avenue.

BOARD IN WEST SEVENTEENTH STREET.—ROOM, on second floor, to let, with Board, to a gentleman and wife or two single gentlemen House has all the modern improvements Apply at 58 West Seventeenth street

BOARD IN HOBOKEN.—PLEASANT ROOMS, WITH Board, for gentlemen, at No. 1 Hudson Terrace, close to the ferry.

BOARD IN HOBOKEN —HANDSOMELY FURNISHED Rooms, with good Board, are offered to three or four gentlemen, by a private family, on moderate terms; the house is pleasantly situated, very near to the ferry, and has all the modern improvements. Apply at 27 Union place.

BOARD WANTED—BY A GENTLEMAN AND LADY OF retired habits, in a small, quiet family, where there are no other boarders Board for the lady only. A furnished Room, with Bedroom, preferred. Address R. C. S, Herald office, stating terms, which must be moderate.

BOARD WANTED—FOR A LADY AND CHILD, IN the country, within thirty miles of New York, in a private family. Terms must be reasonable. Address or call on E. A. McMurray, 271 Pearl street, New York.

BOARDING.—A GENTLEMAN AND HIS WIFE AND two or three single gentlemen can be accommodated with good Board and well furnished Rooms, also a well furnished Parlor, by applying for two days at 242 Broome street, corner of Ludlow.

BOARDING —FURNISHED ROOMS, WITH OR WITHout Board, for gentlemen or ladies, at No. 9 Amity street, near Broadway.

BOARDING.—A FEW GENTLEMEN OR A GENTLEman and wife can be accommodated with good Board, where there would not be more than six or eight boarders, with most pleasant Rooms, and where the comforts of a home may be enjoyed. Terms moderate. Location 464 Eighth avenue, between Thirty-fourth and Thirty-fifth streets.

BOARDING.—A SMALL PRIVATE FAMILY CAN ACcommodate a gentleman and wife, or one or two single gentlemen, with a neatly furnished Room, on the second floor, and Board. The location of the house is fine, a few doors west of Sixth avenue. References exchanged. 88 West Thirteenth street

BOARDING —SINGLE AND MARRIED GENTLEMEN will find handsomely furnished Rooms, in a house with all the modern improvements in the immediate vicinity of

PARLORS with extension room, to let, with or without board Very desirable location, nearly opposite Washington squa. House contains all the modern improvements. Apply No. 5 West Washington place.

FURNISHED FRONT ROOMS—ON SECOND A third stories, with full or partial Board, for two sing gentlemen. All the modern improvements in the house. A ply at 228 East Broadway.

FURNISHED ROOMS.—TO LET, FURNISHED OR U furnished a very pleasant Room and Bedroom on fi floor, fireplace and closet attached, in a private house, No. West Twenty-ninth street Terms moderate.

FURNISHED ROOMS.—A PRIVATE FAMILY, OF TW persons, would let three Rooms on first floor, communicating to a party of gentlemen, or a gentleman and wife f housekeeping, Apply at 402 Fourth street, Albion place.

GENTLEMEN AND THEIR WIVES, OR FAMILIE can be accommodated with furnished Rooms, in suit separate, at 178 West Fourteenth street; also single gent men; reference required; dinner at 6

GRAMERCY PARK, 80 EAST TWENTY-FIRST STREE To let, suits of furnished Rooms, on second and th floors, suitable for families or single gentlemen; house fi class; location very desirable for summer residence, betwe Lexington and Fourth avenues.

HARMONY HALL, 17 CENTRE STREET Gentlemen can be accommodated with nicely furnish Rooms, by the single night or week; rooms all newly fitt up. Apply as above.

HANDSOMELY FURNISHED ROOMS TO LET TO L dies, without board, at 220 Sullivan street, near Amity

HOBOKEN.—ONE OR TWO GENTLEMEN CAN O tain Furnished Front Rooms, having a splendid view the river, with partial Board, in the most delightful part the city, within four minutes' walk of the ferry. Apply No. 6 River terrace.

HOME COMFORTS—VERY DESIRABLE ROOM with Board, can be had at 161 East Eighteenth street, gentlemen and their wives and single gentlemen; no obje tion to children; location excellent.

LARGE, DESIRABLE NEWLY FURNISHED ROOM to let, with Board, at 384 East Fourth street; locati central, one block from Broadway; references exchanged.

MRS. M. B. SUMNER, No. 22 WEST TWENTY-NINTH STREET. A Parlor on first floor, and two single Rooms to let, wi Board. Table and style of housekeeping unexceptionable.

NO. 56 EAST TWENTIETH STREET, CORNER (Fourth avenue, second door from Gramercy Park let. Handsomely furnished Rooms in suits or single, wi private table or without Board; a pleasant location for ge tlemen who prefer taking their meals at a hotel.

NEW YORK BOARD AGENCY, 62 EAST FOURTEEN street, Union square.—Persons wishing Rooms, with without Board, directed without charge Those having roo to let should register them at once.
E. LAWRENCE & CO.

NO. 77 EAST FIFTEENTH STREET, NEAR IRVIN place—Suits or single Rooms to let, with Board, fu nished or unfurnished. House first class; location desirab within one minute's walk of Union square, the Academy Music and the Medical College.

ONE OR TWO GENTLEMEN CAN HAVE SUPERIO accommodations in a private family of young peopl up town, on very moderate terms, to agreeable parties; hou first class; modern improvements. Address, with referenc Broadway, box 196 Herald office.

PERSONS DESIROUS OF OBTAINING GOOD BOAR and pleasant Rooms can be accommodated by applyin at No. 77 Fourth avenue, near Tenth street, one block fre